The Beggar King and the Secret of Happiness

To Liz Edgan—
May you Always find Blessing!
And pass off stories on!
In Peace,

CAL-DAY
April 12.
2008

The
Beggar King
and the
Secret of Happiness

by Joel ben Izzy

ALGONQUIN BOOKS OF CHAPEL HILL

2003

Published by
ALGONQUIN BOOKS OF CHAPEL HILL
Post Office Box 2225
Chapel Hill, North Carolina 27515-2225

a division of
Workman Publishing
708 Broadway
New York, New York 10003

Jack Riemer's piece on Itzhak Perlman first appeared in the
Houston Chronicle, February 10, 2001. Used by permission.
Printed in the United States of America.
Published simultaneously in Canada by Thomas Allen & Son Limited.
Design by Anne Winslow.

Library of Congress Cataloging-in-Publication Data
ben Izzy, Joel.
    The beggar king and the secret of happiness /
Joel ben Izzy.—1st ed.
      p. cm.
    ISBN 1-56512-290-9
    1. ben Izzy, Joel. 2. Storytellers—Biography. 3. Folklorists—
Biography. 4. Jews—Folklore. I. Title.
GR55.B36A3 2003
808.5'43'092—dc21
    [B]
                                      2003052453

10 9 8 7 6 5 4 3 2

For Taly

"In the world of stories, nothing is lost."

—Isaac Bashevis Singer

oo

Contents

oooooooooooooooooooooooooooooooooooooooooooooooooooooooo

The Beggar King and the Secret of Happiness

The Beggar King

LET ME TELL YOU a tale of long ago, from the old city of Jerusalem, back in the days when Solomon was king. He had reached the height of his power and was known throughout the world for his wisdom. With it, he had brought Jerusalem to a golden age. He was the happiest of men and might well have remained so, had it not been for a strange dream.

It came to him, one sweltering night. In it he saw the door to his chamber open and felt a cool breeze. A moment later, in came his long-dead father, King David. The elder king spoke to his son from the world beyond, telling him of the celestial Jerusalem, identical in every regard to the earthly city, but for a single difference—in the center of the city stood a magnificent temple.

"And you, my son, must build such a temple." He described the building in great detail, even as to the size and shape of its stones, as Solomon listened in awe. "One last thing, which is most important," added King David. "You must build it using no metal, for metal is used in forging weapons of war, and this is to be a temple of peace."

"But father," asked Solomon, "how am I to cut the stones without using metal?"

His father did not answer, but suddenly vanished, and the dream ended.

The next morning Solomon called his advisers together, recounting the strange dream and announcing his plans to build the temple, just as his father had described. When he told them he wished to cut the stones without metal, they were as mystified as he.

Only one—Beniah, his most trusted adviser—offered a suggestion. "Your father once spoke of a tiny worm called the Shamir. Though no larger than a grain of barley, it was said that this worm could split through stone. In fact, this was the worm that had been handed by God to Moses, to carve the Ten Commandments."

"Where would I find this worm?" asked Solomon.

"It has not been seen for many years, your highness." Beniah paused. "Not since it came to be in the possession of Ashmodai, the King of the Demons."

A hush fell over Solomon's court, for all knew of the power of the demon king. Only Solomon was not afraid. "Very well, then," he said. "I shall summon Ashmodai!"

Solomon looked from their frightened faces to the ring he wore on his right hand. A simple gold band, it had been given to him by his father, and had great powers, for it was inscribed with the secret name of God. Solomon had used this ring to summon demons before, lesser demons. But never had anyone summoned the great King of the Demons, who lived at the far end of the world, where the mountains were made of copper and the sky was made of lead.

Those in the court drew back, as Solomon twisted his ring. Suddenly, a huge ball of fire appeared before him, and when the flames died down, there stood Ashmodai. All were amazed at what they saw, for the demon king stood fully eight feet tall, with glistening blue skin. He had the feet of a chicken, the wings of an eagle, the head of a lizard, and the personality of a jackass.

"Well, well! If it isn't King Solomon!" he said, his voice as slippery as his skin. "The great, the wise, and the powerful! Even so, he is not content with the size of his kingdom, but must intrude upon the realm of darkness as well. Tell me, your highness, why have you summoned me?"

"I want the worm known as the Shamir, so I may use it to cut the stones for my temple."

"Is that all?" asked Ashmodai. "Then here it is!" he said, producing a small, leaden box. "Now, I demand you release me!"

"No," said Solomon. "Not yet. I shall keep you chained up here for the seven years it will take me to build the temple, to prevent you or any other demons from causing mischief. After it is done, I will ask you one question, and only when you answer it shall I set you free."

"A question for me from the wise King Solomon?" mocked Ashmodai. "And what might that question be?"

"I must think of it."

"Very well, then," answered Ashmodai. "I shall be here, waiting."

WITH ASHMODAI IN the palace, strange things began to happen. Solomon returned from supervising the building of the temple one day to find that all the pillars in the palace had turned to trees, their boughs filled with greenery and ripe, luscious fruit—figs, oranges, and pomegranates. Another night he looked up to see gold coins falling like rain from the domed ceiling of the palace, only to disappear the instant they touched the ground. Sometimes Solomon would hear sweet strains of music, yet when he tried to listen, there was nothing. Ashmodai was a master of illusion, and these illusions Solomon found endlessly fascinating—and infuriating, for they defied his understanding of the world. Each time he found himself fooled, Solomon felt as though his crown were missing a jewel. So, after seven years, when the temple was completed and perfect in every detail, Solomon spoke to Ashmodai.

"Now, as promised, I shall ask you a question, and only when you answer it shall you be free. For all these years, I have watched your illusions. As a great judge, I am often called upon to distinguish between reality and illusion. Now, all I ask is this: What can you teach me about illusion?"

With this, Ashmodai laughed such a wild, maniacal laugh that it echoed through all of Jerusalem. "Illusion!" he cackled. "The great, wise king, who has nothing better to do than torment demons, wishes to learn about illusion? Oh, no, your highness. That would be unthinkable, absurd, impossible—" Suddenly Ashmodai stopped, a grin spreading across his lizard face. "Unless—of course—you would be willing to remove your ring?"

"My ring?" said Solomon. "Remove my ring?"

Solomon looked at the ring, remembering his father's words. "As long as you wear it," he had said, "you will be protected. If you remove it, even for an instant, there is no telling what will happen."

And now, here stood Ashmodai, taunting him. "Yes, Solomon. If you wish to learn what I know of illusion, you must remove your ring."

"That is out of the question!" said Solomon.

"Very well, then, you shall not learn the secrets of illusion from me."

"Then I'll not set you free!"

"That's quite alright. Time means nothing to me—unlike kings, demons live forever. I am content to wait." He slumped down in his chains and began humming to himself.

Desperately curious to hear what Ashmodai had to say, Solomon thought for a time, and finally consulted his advisers. All agreed that it was a bad idea to remove his ring. One even went so far as to say it would be unwise.

"Unwise!" shouted Solomon. "You dare to tell me what is wise? I am the great King Solomon, known throughout the world for my wisdom!"

"That's right, your highness," added Ashmodai. "Why should someone as wise as yourself listen to them?"

Solomon's advisers remained silent, as afraid of the king as they were of Ashmodai. Their comments would have been useless, for Solomon had made up his mind. "I shall remove my ring," he said, "just long enough to hear your answer."

Solomon had Ashmodai placed at one end of the palace, surrounded by twenty-four guards, while he himself stood in the opposite corner.

"Yes, Solomon," said Ashmodai. "Remove your ring!"

Slowly Solomon slid the ring from his finger. For a moment, nothing happened. Then, a gentle breeze began to blow through the palace. Soon it grew stronger, turning to fierce gusts of wind. As Solomon watched, he realized in horror that the wind was coming from the wings of Ashmodai. Each time he flapped them, he doubled in size, from eight feet to sixteen feet to thirty-two feet, until he towered to the ceiling of the palace, breaking free of his chains, his laughter shattering the glass in the windows.

"You fool, Solomon! You should never have removed your ring!" He reached down and plucked the ring from Solomon's hand, then threw it out of a tiny window of the palace. The ring sailed over the city of Jerusalem, beyond the distant hills, past mountains and oceans, finally landing at the far end of the world.

"And now, Solomon, it's your turn! Say good-bye to your kingdom!" With these words, he picked the king up by the shoulders and hurled him through a window on the other side of the palace. Solomon sailed over his beloved city, beyond the hills, over the sea for many hours until, at last, he landed in the midst of a vast desert.

There he lay for some time, every part of his body aching, his mouth parched. He pulled himself up and began walking aimlessly, first this way, then that, until, as the sun set, he came upon a pool of water. He knelt down to drink and there saw something that sent a jolt of terror through him — his reflection.

His crown, which had been a gift from the creatures of the sea, covered with every known precious gem, was gone. His beautiful robe, which he'd been given by the wind, was now in shreds, and looked to be nothing more than rags. And his face, which had been the most handsome in all Jerusalem, was now that of a weathered old man.

Thus it was, lost and unknown, that Solomon began his wanderings. Never could he have imagined the twists and turns his road would take as he struggled, in vain, to return to his beloved Jerusalem. It was a journey that would take him great distances and last a lifetime . . .

I AM NO KING SOLOMON, nor do I claim his wisdom. My voyage was not that of a king, but of a husband, a father, and a teller of tales. Even so, like Solomon, in the story I had told so often, I found myself in a place I never expected to be, in a life I no longer understood.

My journey carried me into the world of stories. There I learned of the tricks they play upon us, bubbling up through the depths of time to teach us their lessons, guide us, and, if we let them, heal us. I also learned how they can fool us, especially when we think we know them well, how they can cleverly hide their truths in places too obvious to see. Some of these truths I stumbled over, coming across the same lessons Solomon must have found in his travels, lessons that can only be learned from loss.

I'll share those truths I found as I tell you my tale, which is itself a true story. But first, let me say what I mean by "truth." I use the word as storytellers do, the way my old teacher, Lenny, once spoke of truth. He had just told me a most amazing story—about a golden retriever he'd once owned and a blue '67 Mustang convertible—and I asked him if it was true.

"True?" he snapped. "What do you mean by 'true'? You want to know if it happened, word for word, exactly as I told it? Makes no difference. You may as well ask me if it's a good story, because a good story is true, whether it happened or not. And a bad story—even if it happened—is a lie.

"The question," he added with a grin, "is not whether the story is *true*, but whether it has *truth* inside it, the kind with a capital T. And that is a mystery only time can solve. But I'll warn you, Joel—never be such a horse's ass to think that just because you can tell a story, you've found all its truth. There are stories in this world that need to rattle around inside your brain for twenty years before they reveal a final, hidden grain of truth."

Lenny had collected many such grains over the years and they stuck to him, like grit to sandpaper, which may account for his personality. Yet his warning comes to mind whenever I use the word "truth."

That said, I'll tell you my tale essentially as it happened, though I will change some parts along the way, for that is what we storytellers do. Yet, as you read this book, you may find some things that strike you as flat-out unbelievable. I know, for that is just how they struck me when they happened. These are things I could not have made up, and so I'll leave them unchanged. As

Mark Twain said: "Truth *is* stranger than fiction . . . Fiction is obliged to stick to possibilities; Truth isn't."

With that, sit back and let me tell you my tale, of a journey that took me through dark times, yet gave me a gift that I treasure. That gift is this story, which I now pass on to you— a tale of lost horses and found wisdom, of buried treasures and wild strawberries, of the beggar king and the secret of happiness.

STORY ORIGIN: CHINA

The Lost Horse

L ong ago in a village in northern China, there lived a man who owned a magnificent horse. So beautiful was this horse that people came from miles around just to admire it. They told him he was blessed to own such a horse.

"Perhaps," he said. "But what seems like a blessing may be a curse."

One day, the horse ran off. It was gone. People came to say how sorry they were for his bad luck.

"Perhaps," he said. "But what seems like a curse may be a blessing."

A few weeks later, the horse returned. It was not alone. It was followed by twenty-one wild horses. By the law of the land, they became his property. He was rich with horses.

His neighbors came to congratulate him on his good fortune. "Truly," they said, "you have been blessed."

"Perhaps. But what seems like a blessing may be a curse."

Shortly after that his son—his only son—tried to ride one of the wild horses. He was thrown from it and broke his leg. The man's neighbors came to say how sorry they were. Surely, he had been cursed.

"Perhaps," he said. "But what seems like a curse may be a blessing."

A week later, the king came through that village, drafting every able-bodied young man for a war against the people of the north. It was a horrible war. Everyone who went from that village was killed. Only that man's son survived, because of his broken leg.

To this day, in that village, they say, "What seems like a blessing may be a curse. What seems like a curse may be a blessing."

CHAPTER ONE

The Lost Horse

JUST HOW I CAME to be a storyteller is a story in itself, a tale of curses turned to blessings. I certainly wasn't born into the art, though I've met many who were. In a pub at the southernmost tip of Ireland I heard a genuine *seanachie,* who sang the ancient ballads with such resonance that you could hear the ghosts of his ancestors singing the chorus. In the Jewish quarter of Jerusalem I came to know a Hassidic *maggid* who could trace his lineage back to Rabbi Nachman of Bratzlav, the great eighteenth-century mystic teller of tales. And once, on the north shore of Oahu, in Hawaii, I shared the stage with a woman who had been chosen as treasurer of five thousand years' worth of her ancestors' stories.

Me, I had no such credentials, and it always left me feeling a little embarrassed among other storytellers. I had grown up in the least magical place on earth, the suburbs of the suburbs to the east of Los Angeles. Where my family lived there were no movie stars, no beaches — no water of any sort, for that matter. In fact, there was no geography at all, as far as we could tell; though we were told of purple mountains to the north, we could not see them through the smog.

It was called the San Gabriel Valley — not to be confused with "the Valley," which is so well known. Ours was "the Other Valley," a world flat and square, with relentlessly straight streets leading to freeways in every direction. Those freeways led to other freeways which led to still more freeways. As far as I knew, this was the world.

I can't say I grew up in a home filled with stories, either. The truth is, stories take time, and my parents' time was spent trying to keep our world from crumbling, as they struggled against poverty and my father's failing health. We belonged to the descending middle class, and my father had tumbled through a dozen careers in an effort to keep us from falling any further. He dreamed of great things for our family, and when those plans inevitably failed he would shrug off the loss with a joke or a proverb. I suppose these might have grown into longer stories had they not been interrupted, usually by the ringing of the telephone. He would rush to answer it, not wanting to miss that all-important call, the one that would surely make us rich, the one that would get our family off welfare, the one that never came.

As for my mother, she didn't actually tell us stories, but rather referred to them as she drove us around town. "You must have heard the stories about Chelm? You know, the Jewish town of fools?"

"No, we haven't," my brothers and I would say. "Tell us!"

"Chelm," she'd repeat, a dreaminess in her voice coming through the guttural sound of the word. "You must have heard about it. It's in Poland. Where it snows all the time. Oh, they were the most wonderful stories."

"Tell us one now!"

"Oh, we used to love them. There was one about the Chelmites building their temple, carrying logs down from the top of a mountain—but I'm no storyteller," she would apologize. "Your Grandpa Izzy was. We could sit and listen to him for hours." She would then trail off, leaving a picture in my mind of Grandpa Izzy, the great storyteller from the faraway city of Cleveland. Years later, when I began telling stories, I would take his name for my own—Joel ben Izzy, Hebrew for "Joel, son of Izzy." But I did not know that at the time. All I knew was that something magical was missing and in its stead we had smog. We rolled up our windows to keep it out, and the station wagon became a vacuum, filled with untold stories, winding its way through the endless suburbs.

It was the absence of magic that sent me looking for it, and I remember the day I found it. I must have been about five. My two older brothers were at school and I was in the supermarket with my mother. I could see she was miserable. Though I didn't know it, she had just learned that my father would need to go to the hospital for another operation, this one for his cataracts. I wanted some way to make her happy, and I found it in the produce section.

"Mommy," I said. "Look over there! That eggplant—it looks like Nixon!"

The resemblance was indeed amazing—with the top of the eggplant curled over like his nose—but not nearly so amazing as my mother's face, which lit up with laughter. What a wonderful thing to make her laugh, to pull her out of her misery, if only for a moment. A few words, and the darkness went away. I started collecting jokes and telling them to her whenever I could. It worked with my father, too, and when I managed to make him laugh, what came out was hearty and full, the laughter of a healthy man. Then I would laugh, and it was at these times I felt close to him.

I became a performer for my parents, doing puppet shows and comic routines. I told jokes and stories in the hospital when my father was there, and every night at bedtime, to my mother. She would come into my room, sit on the bed, exhausted from her life. "Joel," she would say, "tell me a story."

I had no idea that I had found my life's work. But I did know that I loved telling stories to my mother. I told of a world far beyond the one we knew, a land with smogless skies, where poor people became rich and sick people became healthy. With each story that world became more real to me; I could see it reflected in my mother's eyes. And I knew it was that world to which I would someday escape.

JEWISH CULTURE IS RICH with curses—"May you grow like an onion, with your head in the ground and your ass in the air." "May you live like a chandelier—hang by day and burn by night." "May all your teeth rot and fall out but one, and in that one may you have the toothache from hell." Of all the curses I've heard, though, the strangest may well be this one: "May you do what you love for a living." Indeed, it sounds not like a curse at all, but the title of a self-help book that would sell well where I live, in Berkeley. Yet I had come to understand it, in the many years it had taken to turn my love of stories into a livelihood. "Traveling storyteller" isn't exactly a can't-miss career choice, and more than once I'd found myself ready to give it up. Stuck in the rain, with no money and no work, in Manchester. Sick and unable to work in Tel Aviv. Broke and burned out in the subways of Tokyo, wondering what the hell I was doing. Then a voice inside my head would say, "For God's sake, Joel, why can't you get a real job, something that pays? How about law school?" It wasn't the voice of my parents; on the contrary, they loved my stories and were thrilled that I had gone off to chase my dreams. No, it was simply the voice of reason.

Time and again I would bump and skid down to what I thought was the bottom, and just when it seemed things couldn't get any worse, they did. Yet even as the tentacles of despair began to tighten around me, something would always come up—usually the next gig. And when I got there, I had a story to tell. Therein lay the beauty of my profession; whatever did not kill me made for a story, and as long as I could tell that story, all was well.

With that discovery, the work began to roll in, and I found myself able to pursue another dream, one so near to my heart that I had scarcely let myself consider it. I would marry a wonderful woman and raise a family. Our children would know a childhood as different as could be from my own, with healthy parents and money in the bank, far from the suburbs I had known. They would grow up in a home filled with magic, laughter—and stories.

The wonderful woman showed up one night at a party, where I was telling stories. I fell in love as soon as I saw her. She liked me, too, I could tell. But she had dreams of her own, and in none of them had it ever occurred to her that she might hitch her fortunes to that of a traveling storyteller. This was clear from the first words she spoke to me.

"So, what's your real job?"

Her name was Taly, and winning her over took three years and everything I had. It wasn't just my offbeat career choice; adept as I was before a crowd, I floundered miserably when it came to intimate relationships. Joan Baez said it best: "The easiest kind of relationship for me is with ten thousand people. The hardest is with one." Like so many men, I had no idea how to talk about my feelings. Over the next three years, I learned a great deal about how to be with someone, not as a member of my audience, but as a friend and partner, and we turned our attraction into a marriage.

It was not easy at first; anyone who has been married knows that it takes work. But we did the work, and as we did, our love grew. We settled into a hundred-year-old redwood house, tucked away in the hills behind the UC Berkeley campus. And it was there, on the back porch, that we sat on a beautiful afternoon in early spring, watching our son and daughter, who were trying to rake up the leaves as they fell from the oak trees in the yard. The first of that year's freesias had just opened, and the air was filled with the scent of their yellow blooms. I looked around, took a deep breath, and suddenly realized that I had made it. That's when I whispered the words.

"Now I am completely happy."

I don't even think Taly heard me. If she had, she would have responded by spitting three times, the traditional Jewish gesture to keep away the evil eye. But I wasn't worried about the evil eye, or anything else. Nothing could stop me, I believed. When I donned my gray fedora, I could talk any curse into a blessing.

You see, I thought I had found the secret of happiness. And I planned on being happy for a very long time.

"PEOPLE MAKE PLANS and God laughs." That's what my father used to say. The Yiddish expression was a favorite of his, one I heard him say at least a thousand times. Still, I must have missed something. Otherwise I would not have been foolish enough to announce my happiness.

It was the morning after my statement that God saw fit to laugh. The day was Purim, appropriately enough, the Jewish holiday that celebrates twists and turns of fate. The story behind the day tells of an evil man who had plotted to kill all the Jews, but failed to realize that the queen was Jewish. In the end, he meets his death on the very gallows he had built for others, while everyone else celebrates. In that sense it's a classic Jewish holiday: "They tried to kill us. They didn't. Let's eat!"

I awoke that morning from a bizarre dream in which I had climbed down the stairs in our house, lifted the piano high above my head, then dropped it onto my right big toe. The strange thing was that, on waking, I found my toe was actually swollen and throbbing with a magnificent pain.

"You'd better call the doctor," Taly said when she saw it.

"Don't be silly. It's nothing."

"Joel, something's wrong. Look at your toe! My God—it looks like it's going to explode! Call the doctor."

"It's nothing."

I had always avoided doctors, having seen more than enough ushering my father to his death. Taly, on the other hand, lives by the motto, "Cancer until proven otherwise." As a result, she makes frequent trips to doctors and almost always comes back with good news.

"Joel, would you call the doctor?" she said again at breakfast, as I finished my oatmeal.

"Look, it's nothing. It'll go away."

"You can barely walk! How can you perform like that?" she asked later, as I was halfway out the door, my storytelling bag in one hand and an armload of Purim costumes in the other, running late to the first of three gigs.

"No problem. I'll tell them the story of Hillel." Hillel was a great Jewish scholar who had once been challenged to explain all the teaching in the Torah while standing on one foot. "Do unto others as you would have them do unto you," he said. "The rest is commentary."

She didn't buy it. With a sigh, I took off my hat, put down the costumes, and stood on both feet, balancing to show I was fine.

Before she could make her point, our two-year-old daughter, Michaela, made it for her. Running up to hug me good-bye, she stepped on my right toe. I howled in pain, dropping to the floor. Taly helped me up and handed me the phone.

The advice nurse heard my story and didn't miss a beat.

"Gout," she said.

"Gout?"

"Gout," she repeated. "It's called the 'rich man's disease.'"

"I know what it's called. My father had it."

Among his constellation of illnesses, gout had always struck me as particularly unfair, precisely because of the moniker. It was a disease from another era, befitting wealthy statesmen in colonial days, back when there was nothing you could do but prop up your foot and moan about King George. Now, I learned from the nurse, there was a pill that would make it go away in a matter of hours. She had a doctor write a prescription, faxed it to the pharmacy, and scheduled a follow-up appointment. I took the pill and, sure enough, the gout vanished as quickly as it came. It has never bothered me since.

I didn't give the gout another thought until June, when I

found myself in a doctor's office for the follow-up appointment. I sat on the paper-covered patients' table, smiling at the doctor, who smiled back at me. He was a soft-spoken Arabic man, with horn-rimmed glasses, who, I saw on his diplomas, bore the name Ishmael. I liked him, despite my misgivings about doctors. I've spent hours drinking mint tea and discussing philosophy with Arab merchants in the marketplace in Jerusalem, and his office reminded me of that, except instead of trinkets and rugs, it was filled with brochures on topics like "You and Your Prostate." As neither of us could figure out why I was there, he went to the computer and punched in my record number.

"Gout?" he said. "You have gout?"

"I *had* gout. Once. Last March. It only lasted a day." Once he got to the medical questions, I started to fidget. It was the same in the marketplace, when the topic of "rugs" would inevitably come up.

"Well, as long as you're here, let me examine you." He began to feel my neck.

"I don't think that's my foot," I said, "but you're the doctor." His hand was warm.

"There's nothing to be done about your foot. The gout is gone. But I'm an endocrinologist. Necks are my specialty."

"Good thing you're not a proctologist!" The idea of an exam made me nervous, and I began making jokes. "Say, can I call you Ishmael?"

"Call me what you'd like," he said. He paused at one spot and probed a little deeper, looking away, concentrating on what he was feeling. "Did you know you have a little bump in your throat?"

"I have lots of little bumps in my throat. That's what a throat is."

"But you have an extra bump that shouldn't be here."

"I shouldn't be here, doc, the gout is gone . . ."

I stopped speaking when he opened a drawer and pulled out a tray filled with medical implements that looked like something from a horror film. "Given your age and general health, chances that it's anything to worry about are one in a thousand," he said. "Just the same, I'd like to aspirate it. To be on the safe side."

He held up a hypodermic needle the size of a turkey baster.

"That's your idea of 'the safe side'?"

THERE ARE SOME WORDS life does not prepare you to hear, words like, "You have cancer."

I had heard far too much about the disease as a child, as family friends and relatives were afflicted. Grown-ups spoke of it in hushed tones, and the softer they spoke, the closer I listened. I noticed that women's tumors were described in terms of fruit, men's in terms of sports.

"Did you hear about Cousin Sadie? It was the size of an orange!"

"No!"

"And you know that nice man, Mr. Friedman, with the shoe store? In his stomach. A baseball."

"Oy! Like my Aunt Sophie—a papaya."

But cancer was a disease for other people, older people—sick people, for God's sake. I was thirty-seven and in good health, so it wasn't even a possibility lurking in the corners of my imagination on that hot July afternoon, my son's fifth birthday. I had placed five candles on the cake and was just putting on the sixth for good luck when the phone rang.

"I'll get it!" I said, licking chocolate frosting from my fingers.

"Let the machine get it," shouted Taly from the other room.

"But it's probably my mom," I said, picking it up. "Elijah—remember, Grandma Gladys has trouble hearing, so speak loudly and clearly. Okay?"

"Joel?" It was Ishmael. "I've got news. I'm afraid you're one in a thousand."

He talked for several minutes, but I only absorbed a few words here and there.

". . . papillary thyroid cancer . . ."

". . . partial versus full thyroidectomy . . ."

". . . five years, disease-free survival rate . . ."

Taly had lit the candles and was motioning me to get off the phone. Then she saw the look on my face.

"What's wrong?"

I stared at her blankly, trying to come up with another word for "cancer." Finally, I gave up and brushed the question aside. "Nothing, really. We'll be fine. C'mon — before the candles burn down!"

THAT NIGHT, I TUCKED the kids in and told them their bedtime stories, as always. Then I went downstairs, where I found Taly waiting for me, pacing.

"Joel, what is it?"

I thought humor might be the best way to break the news to her. "Do you remember that line in *When Harry Met Sally*? Where Billy Crystal says, 'Don't worry, it's just one of those twenty-four-hour tumors'?"

Her face went pale. "A tumor? Cancer? You have cancer?"

"Just a little cancer. Thyroid cancer. But the doctor said that if you have to have cancer, this is a good kind to have."

She looked baffled. "Good cancer? What are you talking about?"

I fumbled for an explanation, but the words would not come. Looking in her eyes, I could see she was terrified, but she tried to comfort me.

"But it will be okay," she said, nodding. "Won't it?" I nodded back. "This is treatable, right?" Cancer had long been her greatest fear. "You'll be alright. And we'll be alright. Right?"

"That's right," I assured her, regaining my footing. "A blip on the radar screen, nothing more."

Surfacing from general anesthesia felt a bit like waking up with jet lag after a long trip. For a moment I lay there, my eyes closed, no idea where I was, nothing but that strange disorientation and sense of anticipation that comes with the start of an adventure. Keeping my eyes closed tight, I wondered what world awaited me—Budapest? Katmandu? Shanghai? When I opened them, I noticed the machinery, saw tubes in my arms, and felt pain everywhere.

"Some adventure this is . . ." I started to say. I stopped. Something was wrong.

I tried again. "Some adventure . . ." Nothing came out.

Again and again I tried to say something, anything. I tried to call out for Taly. A wave of panic surged through me and my heart began to pound. And only then did I realize what was happening. It was a dream, of course, nothing more. I'd often had dreams like this, usually before a big performance, where I found myself suddenly unable to talk. I would be standing before a large audience, trying to tell a story, and no words would come out of my mouth.

What a relief. A nightmare, nothing more. I tried to remember what performance it was, but couldn't. So I did the only thing I could do and waited for the dream to end.

All around me I heard hospital sounds. Nurses chatting, machinery beeping, footsteps in the hallway. Every few moments I tried to talk. Nothing but air came out.

It was only as sunlight streamed through the window that I realized I was not dreaming. I was wide awake, but could no longer speak.

My horse was gone.

The Cricket Who Jumped to the Moon

Once, when the world was young, there lived a cricket who dreamed of jumping to the moon. He wanted nothing more than to look down and see the earth. Night after night he jumped as high as he could, occasionally reaching the low branches of a tree, sometimes even the upper ones. But he never came close to the moon.

The other crickets who lived in his valley scoffed at his foolish notion. "The moon?" they laughed. "Ridiculous. Impossible."

Undaunted, he kept on jumping for the moon. Over time, his knees grew weak from too many hard landings. He could no longer jump, nor play his evening songs. The other crickets all told jokes about him. Still, he kept on trying, climbing slowly up the trees until the day he died.

Even after he was gone, the jokes remained. They grew longer, and in time they turned into stories. They were passed from one generation to the next and eventually woven into their songs.

To this day, you can hear them sing of his adventures. "Look!" cricket parents say to their children, "There he is! You can see his face, in the shadows of the moon, watching over us."

So it was, after many years, that his dream came true.

CHAPTER TWO

The Cricket Who Jumped to the Moon

MY FATHER SPENT HIS LIFE chasing dreams. Looking back now, I can see that they were both a blessing and a curse to him—a blessing because they gave him the strength to go on, despite all odds, and a curse because none of them were destined to come true.

Many were the nights he thought he'd captured one dream or another, in the form of a fantastic get-rich-quick scheme, an elixir that would restore his health, or an elaborate invention that would bring him fame, fortune, and, what he wanted most of all—happiness. Yet, time and again, he awoke to find that his hopes had slipped through his gnarled fingers. Then he would respond as he did to all the pain in his life—with a laugh.

"What can you do?" he would say. "People make plans and God laughs." As if for emphasis, he'd look toward heaven, his palms raised, and shrug. I would follow his gaze upward, then look back down at his hands. They fascinated and terrified me, with their knuckles swollen like marbles, fingers hooked like the talons of an owl.

They hadn't always looked that way. At one time, before I was born, they had been lithe and nimble, one dancing along the neck of a violin, the other gently holding the bow. That's how they looked in the photograph I'd seen of him standing tall in his white dinner jacket and black trousers, the violin resting under his chin, on the night he debuted with the Cleveland Symphony Orchestra.

He was in his early twenties when the arthritis began to show. I imagine it was subtle at first, his fingers moving imperceptibly more slowly between the strings. He must have heard it in the music before he ever saw it in his hands. Ankylosing spondylitis, the doctors would later call it, a rare form of the disease that caused the vertebrae of his spine to fuse into a single bone. Over the two-and-a-half decades I knew him, I saw his once tall body bend and twist into the shape of a question mark.

I never heard my father play the violin; by the time I was born the instrument itself was all that remained of his once promising career. Throughout my childhood it sat in its case atop the mantelpiece in our living room. Each in turn my two older brothers and I tried to play it, but none of us had the knack. We put it back, and it lay there, gathering dust, until he died.

As a child I did not understand his disease, or why it was that, as I grew taller, he grew shorter. With each trip to the hospital, he came back less able to walk—first with the cane, then the braces, then the walker. When he did walk, he moved so slowly that it was painful to watch. But, as with every other setback in life, he answered with a laugh.

"You know, the bumblebee can't fly," he announced once when he came home from the hospital, this time with a walker. "It's true. The laws of aerodynamics have proven that his wingspan can't support the weight of his body. Good thing for the bumblebee, though, he doesn't follow those laws, and goes on flying just the same."

My father had dozens of such sayings, words of wisdom that would become the legacy he left to my brothers and me. He'd say them whenever he met with failure and then go on chasing the next dream.

After giving up the violin, he had become an inventor, pouring our family's savings into one scheme or another. During the late 1960s he invested in what he thought would be the wave of the future—glow-in-the-dark plastics and paints. Like the remnants of all his other inventions, they littered the house. But by night, they glowed. Spilled paint was everywhere, even on the ceiling, like stars in the sky. That was my father—a rich man in the world of dreams, but poor again when daylight came.

"You know what they say, don't you?" he once asked me. "People make plans . . ."

". . . and God laughs," I answered dutifully, handing him a brick. I sat on his bed and he sat on a folding chair in the bathroom doorway, attached to one of his inventions. It was a device that was supposed to straighten out his back, using rope slung over a chin-up bar, with a neck brace on one end and a soup pot on the other. It was my job to hand him bricks. Each time he placed another in the pot he would grimace in pain, then force himself to smile, looking for all the world like he was trying to hang himself.

"But I don't get it," I said. "You say God laughs whenever something bad happens. Why? What's so funny?"

He stopped for a moment, brick poised in midair.

"You want to know why?"

I nodded.

He shrugged, the pot full of bricks bobbing up and down. "I don't know. You'll have to ask someone wiser than me. But here's what I do know. In this life you have a choice. You can laugh along with God, or you can cry all alone. Now, which are you going to do?"

So I learned to laugh along with my father.

. . .

THE WEEKS WENT BY with no sign of my voice, and I found myself thinking more and more about my father. I tried to remember his laughter, and tried not to think about his fingers. There was a difference, I told myself; his loss was permanent. Mine was temporary.

That's what the doctor thought. "It's your vocal nerve," he'd said when he heard my quiet, breathy whisper. "Must still be in shock. But I wouldn't worry about it. They usually come back. Give it a couple weeks, maybe as long as a month. Two at the very most."

That's how Taly explained it to the kids, as a temporary loss, the day I came home from the hospital.

"Elijah, Michaela, listen to me," she said. They ignored her, each one clinging on to one of my legs in a welcome-home embrace, as they pelted me with questions.

"Did it hurt? Did they take out that thing in your neck? Can we see it? Were you brave? Tell us the story!"

"Kids," she said, "I need to tell you something. Something important." They finally stopped and looked up at her. "Your daddy can't talk."

Michaela's face took on a puzzled expression; Elijah looked betrayed, and shook his head. "Yes he can," he finally said. "He talks all the time. Right, Daddy?" He looked to me for confirmation. I nodded back toward Taly.

"No," she said, "I'm afraid he can't. His 'owie' is gone, and that's the most important thing. But, for now, he can't talk. But it's just for a while. Right, Joel?"

I nodded.

"How long, Daddy?" asked Michaela.

"Pretty soon," Taly answered. "But we don't know exactly when. Until then he's supposed to rest his voice, so he can only whisper, just a tiny bit."

"And when it comes back, you'll tell us stories?" asked Elijah.

I couldn't hold back.

"Lots and . . . lots of . . . stories."

NEITHER OF THE CHILDREN quite knew what to make of their almost mute father. At first Michaela thought it was funny, a kind of running gag, because of the strange, improvised sign language I tried to use to communicate with her. I whispered only when I absolutely had to, partly because to do so stung my throat and partly because whenever I did, she screwed up her face and shook her head. "Daddy, talk louder!"

For Elijah my missing voice meant a new job. When I was with Taly, she spoke on my behalf. But since she was working long hours to make up for some of my lost income, Elijah became my voice. As my whisper could not be heard over any other noise—the sound of a passing car, background music, or a plane flying overhead—he would come with me on errands. When I had something to say, I would whisper the words in his ear, then lift him up so he could repeat them aloud: "My daddy would like change for a twenty."

At first we were both excited about his new role. This was a good thing, I told myself, a father and son bonding, having adventures. He did his job well, but I began to notice that the attention from strangers was hard for him. Always on the shy side, he drew back from shopkeepers, grocery baggers, bank tellers, all of whom commented on how cute he was. One even asked if I was a ventriloquist. Elijah handled it stoically, but I could tell he was embarrassed, not just for his sake, but for mine. Sensing this, I tried to speak up whenever I could, but my whispers made it worse. He did not want people to know that there was something wrong with me.

Hard as it was for him in public, it was tougher still when we were alone. He had entered that age of endless questions, when the world is one big mystery and your parents know all the answers. I had looked forward to this time since before he was born. But now, as the questions came, I scrambled to answer them.

"Daddy, why is there a dragon on the Welsh flag? Or is it a griffin? What's the difference? What is mythology? You once told me a story about a troll. Where do trolls live? Can you speak French? How does time work? What's a ventriloquist? Why can't you talk?"

In response to each question, I squeezed out a word or two,

then tried to fill the rest in with gestures. I drew on napkins. I pulled books off shelves and pointed to pictures. He would nod appreciatively and then, a moment later, ask another question, and the whole process would start over.

A MONTH AFTER the surgery, Taly's worry began to show. Though she tried to hide her concern, especially in front of the kids, it came out in the morning, when we awoke.

"Do you feel anything? A twitch?" The doctor had said that I might feel a slight twinge or a tingle before the nerve came back to life.

I shook my head.

"How about now?" she would ask again, five minutes later.

"Don't worry," I whispered. "It will . . . be all . . . right." With my breathy whisper, I could only get out a word or two before I had to stop for breath.

"But I am worried. I'm worried about you. What if your voice doesn't come back?"

"My father . . . used to say . . . that ninety- . . . five percent . . ." I stopped, out of breath. I'd meant to repeat another of his sayings, that ninety-five percent of the things we worry about never come to pass, which shows that worrying is a very effective means of dealing with problems. But it missed the mark.

"Yes," she said. "I was thinking about your father."

She didn't say another word, but we'd been together long enough that she didn't have to. Though Taly had never met my father, she had heard enough of his life story to see it as a worst-case scenario for mine.

I found myself thinking of my father often, and of one story in particular—a joke, really—that he used to love, about a man who goes to a tailor to order a new suit. The tailor takes measurements and tells him to come back the next week. The man does, but when he tries on the suit, it fits terribly.

"What is this?" he says. "This sleeve is way too long and the other is too short. And the pants are tight on this side and baggy on the other!"

"Relax," says the tailor. "The suit is fine. Look." He leads the man to the mirror. "You've got to bring your right shoulder back, like so. Then tilt your head to the side. That's right. Now lean like this, with your left foot forward. . . . Perfect!"

"Okay," says the man, scrunching before the mirror. "Yeah, I see. It looks good." He slouches back and hobbles out of the shop and onto the street, where two women notice his strange walk.

"My God!" says one. "What happened to him?"

"I don't know," says the other. "But that's a great-looking suit!"

I'd heard him tell it many times over the years. He especially loved acting out the part of the customer, and I loved watching him until one day, when I was about fifteen, I realized that his body looked no different when he was done acting out the character. He had become that man in the suit. It wasn't just his body; it was his whole life, twisted around to avoid seeing his failure.

As he neared death, his visions of success grew more vivid. In one of my last visits with him, in a nursing home, he motioned for me to come close, then pointed to the top of a closet. "See those three guys up there?" he whispered. "They're Turkish coffee merchants. And we've just signed a deal—a big one. But it's not for coffee, it's for cheese! We're rich! But keep it a secret. . . ."

I nodded, loving him for who he was. Even so, I made two promises to myself. One was that I would never let myself be deluded into thinking I had succeeded. The other was that I would not fail.

THE ONLY THING between me and happiness, I decided, was my lost voice. Some evenings, after Taly and the kids had gone to bed, I would go down to my office, a beautiful redwood-paneled room, which has long been my place of refuge. I had filled it with puppets and masks that I had collected on my travels, and on one wall I'd hung a huge map of the world, with pins and yarn marking the places I'd been and the stories I'd found. At night my office would be silent, and in this silence I would sit, awaiting the return of my voice.

Sometimes I would imagine energy flowing to my throat, the nerve suddenly springing to life.

It was on one of these nights, as I sat in this meditative state, convinced I was on the verge of success, that the phone rang. I jumped up and very nearly answered it. But I managed to hold myself back, then cringed as I heard, yet again, the message I'd recorded months earlier: "Hi! Joel here. Can't talk now—I'll call you back when I can!" Beep.

I waited for the caller's voice, knowing it would be someone offering to pay me money to do the one thing I could not do.

"Hi Joel! We're big fans of yours here in San Francisco. Look, we've got a bar mitzvah coming up next month, gonna be one hell of a party. We got a DJ and a magician and you would be the icing on the cake. I know it's not much notice, but for what it's worth, you can name your price . . ."

The machine clicked off and I sat there, in its echo, staring at the map. I did not want to think about the money lost from that gig, or about all the other gigs I'd canceled. Instead, with my future now a question mark, I turned to thinking about my past. My eyes traced the yarn on the map from pin to pin. Budapest. Hong Kong. Rome. As I looked at each one, a place came to life, filled with people, smells, tastes, and sounds, reminding me of the stories I had told and loved. The stories led me backward in circles, over the years, all the way to where my career had begun, not far from Berkeley, just outside of Santa Cruz, which was marked by a pin with a bright yellow head.

ALL STORYTELLERS REMEMBER the teller who first inspired them; it leaves a lifelong impression. In storytelling circles, this person is known as a teller's "mama duck." Lenny was my mama duck.

I'd first heard him telling stories one night at a pub, nearly twenty years earlier, in downtown Santa Cruz. I'd seen a flyer on the door and walked in, with no idea what to expect. He stood alone, in silence, on a platform in a corner of the room. His appearance was not particularly striking—somewhat stocky, with a beard and bushy hair. He looked no more like a storyteller than anyone else in the bar.

Yet when he opened his mouth, everything changed. The room fell into complete silence, and I found myself transported, first to a crumbling castle in the Scottish highlands, then to a schoolhouse in New England, and finally to a tiny village in Eastern Europe. There I met and fell in love with characters painted by his words, people more real to me than many I knew. I left at the end of the evening, nostalgic for places I'd never been and missing people I'd never met, knowing I had found my life's work.

The next day I found out where he lived and rode my bike ten miles through the redwoods to his cabin, where I begged him to be my teacher.

"You?" He laughed as though I'd told a joke. "But you're just a kid! Do you even know *why* you want to tell stories?"

I shrugged, noticing something I had not seen the night before. When he spoke, he gestured using only his right hand.

He shook his head, laughing again. "You're like the guy who goes to the rabbi to study Talmud. You know the story?"

I didn't.

"A young man asks a rabbi to teach him the wisdom of the Talmud. The rabbi tells him he's not ready. The man insists he is, so the rabbi gives him a test.

"'Two burglars climb down a chimney to rob a house,' says the rabbi. 'One's face gets dirty, the other stays clean. Which one washes his face?'

"'The one with the dirty face, of course,' says the man.

"'No,' says the rabbi. 'It's the one with the clean face. Because he looks at the one with the dirty face and assumes that his own face must be dirty. Meanwhile, the one with the dirty face sees the other and assumes that his own face must be clean.'

"'Ah-ha!' says the man. 'Now I understand.'

"'No, you think you understand, but you do not. Try again: Two burglars climb down a chimney to rob a house. Which one washes his face?'

"'The one with the clean face, right?'

"'Wrong again,' says the rabbi. 'If they both go down the chimney, both of their faces get dirty. You see,' says the rabbi, 'you're not ready. Someone like you wastes time looking for answers, when you should be looking for questions.'"

He then closed the door in my face. But I came back the next day, and before he could close the door again I shouted, "Wait! I have a question."

He stared at me, eyebrows raised.

"Since when do burglars stop to wash their faces?"

"Ah!" he smiled. "Now we're getting somewhere."

FOR THE NEXT six months I rode my bike to his cabin twice a week, to sit before his wood-burning stove and listen to him tell tales. He seemed to know every story ever told—as well as all the same jokes my father knew—and when I told him one I'd learned, he already knew three variations of it.

I followed him to all his performances, amazed each time as I watched the effect his words had on the crowd. He seemed to drink in their affection, and mine as well. He called me his star pupil, though I was his only one. One afternoon, when I finally told him a story he had not heard before, he laughed a long, deep laugh, then disappeared into his bedroom. He emerged a moment later with a large box.

"I've been waiting for this," he said, handing it to me.

Inside I found a beautiful gray fedora. It fit perfectly, and I wore it to all my performances.

But Lenny had a dark side, a bitterness that began to creep into our visits. It came out unexpectedly, usually triggered by something I would unknowingly do or say. Then he would turn critical, and sometimes even hostile. One night he showed up late and drunk to a performance I was giving at the community center in downtown Santa Cruz. He stood in the back of the room, shaking his head, and he left early. When I saw him at his cabin the next day, he was hungover, and when I asked him what he thought of my storytelling the night before, he shrugged.

"What do I think? I think I was right. You're no storyteller, just a kid with nothing to say." This, I didn't need. I turned to the door. "Leaving? Good. Come back when you've got a story worth telling."

I walked out without looking back and had not seen him since.

As I NEARED the two-month mark, I became obsessed with the return of my voice, and at Taly's suggestion, I began to see specialists.

They used every manner of contrivance to examine my vocal cords—old-fashioned tongue depressors, high-tech rods with strobe lights. One actually looked up my nose with a rubber hose. As I expected, they all agreed with my surgeon: There was a two-month window in which my voice would either return or not, and there was nothing to do but wait and see.

There was a bright spot, though, something else on which they all agreed. There actually *was* one person who could say, definitively, whether my voice would return. He was the expert among experts, and so much respect did they have for him that they mentioned his name only in whispers, and preferred to write it down, on the backs of their own business cards. The name itself seemed to hold a certain mystique—a long Eastern European name, filled with unlikely consonants and scarcely a vowel, an unpronounceable word that would put an end to a game of Scrabble. He was the one I needed to see.

"THE STORYTELLER HAS ARRIVED!"

I stood up from the couch in the waiting room and turned to see the source of the deep, thickly accented voice. He stood there, one hand holding the tape I'd sent him, the other reaching out to shake mine. He looked the perfect picture of a mad scientist, with silver hair and horn-rimmed glasses, slightly askew, and I liked him instantly.

"Very nice stories!" he said, holding out the tape. "I liked especially the tales of Chelm. These, I have not heard for a very long time. Now, let us see if we can find your voice."

I followed him into his office, which was lined with pictures of celebrities whose voices he had saved, so many photos that it looked like a deli. After motioning me to a stool, he read carefully over my records, then stared down my throat for a very long time.

He looked again at my records, then spoke.

"You wish to know if your voice will return. And if so, when. Correct?"

I nodded.

"I see from your records that it has now been gone two months."

"Only fifty- . . . seven days."

"Eight weeks," he said. "And no movement in your vocal cord. This is not a good sign." He paused, shaking his head, then sighed. "I am afraid the nerve is dead. It will not come back to life. I am sorry. Very sorry."

I stared at him, waiting for something better. After a long time, he spoke again. "This is very hard for you, I know. You are a storyteller, so perhaps it will help you to think of this as a story. What do the sages tell us?" he paused, lifting his eyebrows. "'The voice is the gateway to the soul.' And before that gateway stand two guards—your vocal cords. To make sound they must come together—like two rabbis arguing about Talmud. But in your case, one rabbi is silent. Why? I wish I knew." He paused. Then, leaning in close to me, he whispered.

"Perhaps he knows a secret."

Optimism and Pessimism

There once lived a king who had twin sons. Though they looked exactly alike, their personalities were different as night and day. One was a devout pessimist, the other an incurable optimist.

When they came of age, the king decided it was time to open their eyes to the other side of life. He would do it through the gifts he gave them.

For the pessimist, he went to the royal jeweler.

"I would like him to have the finest watch ever made," he said. "Money is no object. Jewels, diamonds, gold, platinum—the best. And I want it ready by his birthday."

For the optimist, he went to the palace gardener.

"When he wakes up on the morning of his birthday, I want him to see, at the foot of his bed, a huge pile of manure."

So came the birthday. With great anticipation, he went to see his pessimistic son. He found him sitting glumly on his bed, holding a magnificent watch.

"How do you like your gift?" asked the king.

"It's alright," said the pessimist. "But it's really rather gaudy. And even if it wasn't, it's the sort of thing that will probably get stolen, or I might lose it. It might also break . . ."

The king had heard enough and went off to his son the optimist, whom he found dancing with joy. When his father entered the room, the son ran up and hugged him.

"Oh, thank you, father, thank you! It's just what I wanted!"

Perplexed, the father asked the son what he was thanking him for.

"Why, father—for the horse!"

CHAPTER THREE

Optimism and Pessimism

"A DOOR CLOSES, A WINDOW OPENS."

That's what my mother always said to me and my brothers. It's the sort of thing mothers often say, but for her the words became a mantra, recited again and again as doors closed around her. Yet with each slam, she became more optimistic.

She and my father had left Cleveland for sunny Southern California, where she dreamed of starting a new life and pursuing her love of journalism. A born interviewer, she had a gift for asking just the right question and listening between the lines of the answer. Her skills had served her well as a cub reporter for the *Cleveland Plain Dealer*, where she showed a natural ability to draw stories out of people. Once she found a story, she would follow it from the time she found it on the street until the next morning, when the paper rolled off the presses.

Years later, audiologists suggested it was the noise from those presses that caused her hearing loss. The first signs came when my brothers and I were young, as bits of conversation she missed, and in the fights she had with my father. He had trouble turning to face her when he spoke, and she strained to understand his words.

"What's the matter?" he'd shout. "Are you deaf?"

She wasn't, yet, but was well on her way. And as her hearing went, so did her career in journalism. For someone else it would have been a bitter disappointment, but she managed to see the bright side; no longer would she have to hear bad news.

After my father died, her hearing loss became her calling card. She moved to a condominium in Alhambra, east of Los Angeles, and began campaigning for the rights of the hearing impaired. Joining an organization called Self Help for the Hard of Hearing—SHHH!—she even managed to find the humorous side of hearing loss, attending workshops with titles like "What do you say after you say 'What did you say?'" She also began to write again—articles for the organization's newsletter, as well as human-interest features for local newspapers, finding people who would either answer her questions in writing or submit to the grueling process of an interview, in which they would have to repeat each answer several times. I was the subject of many such articles: "Local Boy Travels World, Telling Tales." "Have Stories, Will Travel." "My Son the Storyteller."

Each time I made a new storytelling tape, I would send her a copy. She would sit before her tape recorder, holding the little microphone that hooked up to her hearing aid, struggling to understand. I would give her written transcripts, too, but she wanted to *hear* the stories, and when she picked up a few of the words, after many attempts, she glowed with pride. Sending her the tapes was my part of an agreement we had long honored, but never spoken — the "good-news rule." I only sent her those things that would make her happy and proud — newspaper articles about me, along with photos of Taly and the kids. For her part, she sent me articles she wrote, along with envelopes full of clippings from newspapers and magazines, *schmaltzy* stories she thought would make me smile.

I suppose that's why I hadn't told her about the cancer. It's not that I meant it to be a secret, but it's hard to bring up bad news, and I didn't want to worry her. At first, I had decided to wait until after the operation, then tell her the whole story, in person, the next time I was performing in Los Angeles. Since returning from the hospital, though, I had avoided her calls, waiting for my voice to return. There were many calls I had not returned; both my brothers had phoned wondering why I was so out of touch, and when I didn't answer their calls, they wrote letters.

Friends wrote, too, as did fans, asking what was up with me. But my mother's calls pulled at me.

Then, the day after I'd seen the experts' expert, I was in the kitchen spreading cream cheese on a bagel for Elijah when the phone rang. He picked it up and handed it to me, then sat down to eat his bagel. I stared at the phone for some time before finally whispering a tentative hello.

"Elijah?" she guessed. "This is Grandma Gladys!" Her voice was very loud.

"No, Mom . . . it's me."

"You must be excited about starting kindergarten?"

"Mom, it's not . . . Elijah, it's me!"

"That's good. I bet you'll be a wonderful student. Is your daddy there?"

There was the squeal of feedback, then a long pause as she adjusted her hearing aid. "Hello?" she said. " Just a minute."

Odd as it may seem, this was not such an unusual conversation for us, even when I could speak. She would get flustered because she couldn't hear, and I enunciated until my face hurt. We had not had a good phone conversation in years, and those in person were little better.

"Hello? Elijah?" she said, when she finally came back on the phone.

"MOM!" I whispered as loudly as I could. "IT'S JOEL! YOUR SON!"

"Oh, Joel! Hi. I had such a nice talk with Elijah—he sounds excited about kindergarten. And how are you?"

This was the time to tell her. But I paused, not knowing what to say, and the moment passed.

FALL BROUGHT BIG TRANSITIONS—the start of kindergarten for Elijah and of preschool for Michaela. He boldly marched off to his new school, but she had a tougher time, and her first day ended in tears. The second did, as well, but then, on the third, she jumped out of our arms and dashed into the classroom to play.

With the kids away at school and Taly at work, the days dragged on for me, my waking hours spent hoping, wishing, and praying that the expert had been wrong. Hard as the days were, though, evenings were tougher, my attempts at speech throughout the day having reduced my whisper to near silence.

Bedtime was especially hard. It had always been my special time with the kids—a book, a story, and a kiss goodnight—the ritual that had brought to a close every day they'd ever known. At first Michaela would forget. "Daddy, tell a story! A Chelm story! Or the one about the lost horse! Or the Irish king!"

Then, Elijah would remind her. "No, Michaela. We don't want to hear a story, do we?" She'd look puzzled at first, then shake her head in agreement. "It's okay, Daddy. We don't want to hear a story tonight."

One night I came up with a plan. I chose one of their favorite books, *The Little Engine That Could*. Elijah could very nearly read it, and Michaela had all but memorized it. I hid Michaela's tape recorder under the bed, with one of my tapes cued up. I turned down the lights and we huddled together. Between the two of them, they recited the book, word for word. Then I reached down to the recorder and pressed "PLAY."

"Long ago, in Ireland, there lived a king. He was not a kind king . . . but a mean king, and he decided to play a little trick on his adviser . . ."

Their eyes opened wide. Elijah must have known what I was doing, but he didn't seem to mind. Michaela broke into a huge grin. I lip-synched along, adding gestures and facial expressions, until I got to the ending, when the storyteller must answer the king's riddle: How many stars are there in the sky?

"Your highness, there are exactly forty-seven milllllion, twooo huuuundred aaand eiiiighty-sixxxx thousssssand . . ." My voice came to a garbled stop.

They stared at me, waiting.

"Then what happened?" Elijah asked.

"Daddy, keep going!" said Michaela.

The tape recorder clicked loudly, its batteries dead. They looked up at me, waiting.

"They lived . . . happily ever . . . after."

. . .

I WAS FAR FROM HAPPY. And with each day that passed, what remained of my happiness drained steadily away. Finally, one rainy Saturday afternoon, I drove across the Bay Bridge to San Francisco in a last-ditch attempt to regain some control.

The man who'd left a message on my answering machine had left an e-mail address, and so I'd booked the bar mitzvah gig— for no small fee. I began to regret my choice as soon as I crossed the bridge. Trying to perform was a ridiculous thing to do, driven as it was by my relentless optimism. *You do your best under pressure,* a voice inside me had said. *Maybe, just maybe, your voice will return the moment you get on stage.* Through the pouring rain, I could see the marquis of the swank San Francisco hotel, where the boy's name flashed in bright lights. I'd told stories at wonderful bar mitzvah receptions in my time—beautiful, heartwarming events to mark a coming of age. I could tell that this was not one of them.

As I made my way into the lobby I saw a life-size cutout of the bar mitzvah boy. Above it were the words "The Greatest Bar Mitzvah Ever!" with quotes all around: "Riveting!" "Irresistible!" "Two thumbs up!" This was a movie-star-theme bar mitzvah and, judging from the picture of the boy smoking a cigar and holding an Academy Award, it was his idea.

Techno music spilled from the ballroom into the lobby, and other hotel guests covered their ears as they rushed past. Once inside the room I found blinding strobe lights reflecting off of mirror balls onto gold streamers, gold balloons, and gold lamé. The e-mail had said it would be a "dressy" affair, and I had grudgingly put on the suit I usually reserve for weddings and funerals, which left me feeling underdressed and overdressed at the same time. I began to panic.

As I stood there, a woman in a gold flapper's dress and stiletto heels teetered up to me, sloshing half of her martini out of the glass. "We're so glad you're here! You must be—oh, what's your name? Don't tell me. Izzy? Ben? Joel? You're the storyteller—you're on next, right after the magishishian."

I made my way to the stage. Nearby I could see the bar mitzvah boy, looking much like he did in the poster, the buttons of his tuxedo straining to contain him as he held court. Meanwhile, onstage, the magician wearily linked and unlinked metal rings. It's usually the loudest of magic tricks, but in all the noise, the sound was lost. I watched him a moment longer, and then it came to me. A plan, and a good one. Maybe, I told myself, just maybe, no one would notice me. After all, no one was paying any attention to *him*. That was it. I would simply *mouth* the words.

"They're all yours," he said, as he scrambled offstage, table full of props in one hand, rabbit in the other. I took my place before the microphone, smile on my face, ready to pretend I was telling a story. As for choosing the story, I would go through the same ritual I always did, just before every performance—wait patiently for one to come tap me on the shoulder. Sure enough, along came "The Beggar King," and I launched into my pantomime.

At first it worked like a charm. No one noticed me, and after ten minutes I thought I was home free. Then, something went wrong. It began with the bar mitzvah boy, who I could see staring at me with a quizzical look on his face. He shushed the boy next to him. As they grew quiet, other people began looking at them, then at me. A silence spread through the room. What was happening? The DJ turned off the music. People settled into their chairs, and even the adults at their tables stopped talking. Within a minute the place was dead quiet, with every eye looking right at me.

I watched the expressions on their faces turn from curiosity to bewilderment, thinking how the magician would have loved this response. They leaned forward and squinted, gesturing with their hands as though to extract the words from me. Several people rubbed their ears, worried they'd suddenly gone deaf, and those with hearing aids adjusted them. Others merely stared at me, their heads tilted to one side, curiously attentive. I waited for them to start talking again — after all, how long could they stare at me? — but instead the silence grew louder. There was not even the clink of silverware. Something else overtook them; *en masse,* they became cruelly polite. They were trying to help me, and I could feel their pity flowing up to me in waves. I had no choice but to try telling the story I'd been faking, the microphone amplifying my whispers and gasps.

I was up there for what seemed like hours. Finally I got to the end of the story, grabbed my bag, and took a bow I didn't deserve, to polite applause. The last thing I wanted was to stick around and try to explain why I couldn't talk. Yet no one mentioned it. My scratchy excuse for a voice had become the elephant in the room, that thing no one talks about because it's too obvious. Instead, as I went to collect my check, reeling with guilt, the mother gushed appreciation.

"What charming stories you must have told! Now, where is that husband of mine?" She searched the room, then pointed to a larger version of her son. "Wait right here." She winked. "He has the checkbook."

As I waited, other guests made polite conversation, asking questions I couldn't begin to answer over the noise in the room. "Have you been telling stories long?" one man asked. "Is this your full-time living?" asked another, who looked somewhat concerned. As I did my best to nod and gesture answers to their questions, a frail elderly woman put her hand on my arm. "Your performance was . . ." Her face went blank and I could tell she had forgotten whatever kind words she had been about to say. She smiled, nodded, and began again. "Your performance was . . ."

"Unbelievable!" said a voice behind me. "Absolutely unbelievable!"

I did not have to look to see the face; I knew the voice. It was Lenny.

The Vow of Silence

There was once a man who decided to enter a monastery. On his arrival, he took a vow of silence. He was not to utter a single word for five years, at which time he would be granted a five-minute interview with the abbot.

Five years later, the abbot summoned him.

"What do you have to say of your time here?"

The monk thought for a moment, then said, "At first, I had a problem with the concept of the holy trinity, but have now come to understand it. Also, it has been difficult to awaken each morning at four o'clock, but I have grown used to it."

"Is that all you have to say?" asked the abbot.

The man nodded.

"Very well, our next meeting will be in five years."

Five years later, the man went to see the abbot.

"What do you have to say?"

"Well, it has not been easy to accept the truth of the catechism, but I have done so. Also, it's been hard to be content eating only one bowl of gruel each day."

"Is that all you have to say?"

The man nodded.

"Very well, our next meeting will be in five years."

Five years later, the man went again to see the abbot.

"What do you have to say?"

"It has been a challenge to accept the idea of divine grace, but I have done so. Also, it has been somewhat uncomfortable sleeping on a stone floor with no mattress for all these years, but I have grown used to it."

"Is that all you have to say?"

"No, there is one more thing. I'm leaving the monastery."

"Well, it's about time! You've done nothing but bitch and moan since you got here!"

CHAPTER FOUR

The Vow of Silence

I STOOD THERE, staring at Lenny, amazed by how old he looked. Were it not for his voice, I would not have recognized him. The skin hung loosely from his face, except around his dark, puffy eyes. His once full head of hair was all but gone, and what remained hung down from the sides in long, gray strands that blended with his unkempt beard. But his face beamed.

"What's it been?" he said, counting to himself. "Almost twenty years, and not even a hello?" His voice was loud, and several heads turned to look at us. "I've been looking forward to this. I thought you'd be glad to see me."

I reached out to shake his hand, doing my best to smile and say, "How are you?"

"Would you speak up?" He spoke to the gathering crowd. "I

can't hear a word he's saying, can you?" Turning back to me, he said, "What's with the mumbling? Can't you talk?" As I fumbled for an answer, I was relieved to see the bar mitzvah boy's mother coming toward us.

"Here's the check," she said, giving Lenny a sideways glance, then disappearing. I nodded politely as I took it but, a moment later, Lenny snatched it from my hand. "My God!" he exclaimed, holding the check out at arm's length, his eyes squinting. Then, leaning forward, he whispered, "Am I reading this right? Look at what they pay you! And for what you did up there?"

I'd had enough. I grabbed the check, picked up my story bag, and headed for the door.

"Hey, where are you going?" he called. I could hear him explaining himself to the crowd. "He was my student. I haven't seen him in almost twenty years, and now he doesn't even talk to me!"

Glancing over my shoulder, I could see those around him looking curious and confused, as they had when I'd been on-stage. Leaving him there, I made my way through the lobby, beyond the din of the music and outside into the rain. But a moment later I heard him call. I turned to see him waving one arm at me and limping quickly in my direction.

I had no desire to see Lenny, or anyone else, but there was nothing else to do. I waited until he arrived at my car, out of breath. "Joel, why are you running?" he said. "Here I've been, looking forward to seeing you, and you won't even say 'hello.'"

"Hello," I whispered. He shrugged, waiting for more. "Look, I . . . really can't talk."

"So it seems!" he shouted. He leaned toward me and whispered, "What, is it some sort of secret?" Raindrops splattered off his bald head.

"Lenny," I whispered as loudly as I could, "it's good . . . to see you. You look well. I wish I . . . could stay . . ."

He shook his head. "Joel, you're lying. You can't even talk and you're telling me lies! I look like shit, and you just want to get out of here as fast as you can."

Not knowing what to do, I unlocked the door, went around to the trunk, and loaded my story bag. By the time I closed the trunk, he was gone. My eyes scanned the parking lot and the rain, but in the darkness there was no sign of him. I breathed a sigh of relief and opened the car door. I gasped. He was in the driver's seat.

I stood there looking at him looking up at me. "Well?" he asked. "You going to get in, or stand there, like a turkey in the rain?"

He stared at me in a puzzled way, then a look of understanding came over his face, and he nodded. "Oh. I see. Good point. You'd better drive. They took away my license. This eye—" he pointed to the right one "—completely blind." He climbed over the armrest to the passenger side and motioned me in, patting the seat. It was ridiculous, but I was getting soaked. I climbed into the car, wondering how to get him out.

"Don't worry," he said, as he slid the seat back. "You'll remember when you get there. Just drive." When I didn't respond, he gave an exasperated sigh and said, "Alright, 280 down to Highway 17, south to the Ben Lomond exit, left at the stop sign. Then you go about three miles until you reach the dirt road . . ."

I sat there, awestruck by his nerve. Directions. He hadn't even bothered to ask. He *expected* me to give him a ride. His cabin in Ben Lomond was at least an hour and a half away, more like two in this rain, in exactly the wrong direction.

For a moment I stared at him, and he stared back at me. He made no sign of leaving, and as I sat wondering what to do, it struck me that driving him home might be the easiest way to get rid of him. Besides, how else would he get home? It would be a good deed, I told myself as I started the engine, and perhaps a good deed would turn into good luck, which I could certainly use. Pulling out the cell phone, I called and left a message for Taly, saying I'd be late.

As I drove, Lenny rambled. The bar mitzvah boy, it turned out, was his second cousin, but he couldn't stand the kid, the parents, or the rest of the whole family. "Not a one of them deeper than a puddle. Still," he added, picking at something be-tween his teeth, "the food wasn't bad."

He had gotten a ride to the bar mitzvah with another relative, but had managed to get into a fight with her, which explained why he needed me to give him a ride home. The bar mitzvah boy's mother had called him some months back and asked if he would tell some stories at the reception. "But I'm retired now. Storyteller emeritus. I only tell stories when I want to, and I don't do bar mitzvahs anymore. I knew you lived in Berkeley because of the articles in the papers, so I gave her your name. That's how you got the gig."

He paused here, as though expecting gratitude from me. When I didn't respond, he shrugged and went on talking. This was fine by me; I had nothing to say to him, nor could I have made myself heard over the rain pounding on the roof of the car.

He'd stopped performing publicly shortly after I'd left. Things had not gone well for him. "You catch me at a good time," he said, coughing. "Between heart attacks. January 27 last year was the first one. I don't know when the next will be. Then there's the diabetes. They made me stop drinking. You mind if I take off my shoes? My feet are killing me."

I turned off the highway and found my way to the dirt road that wound through the woods to his cabin. He'd been right about one thing; I did remember the road as I got closer, and I thought back to the anticipation I'd once felt, riding my bike through the fog to his cabin on summer afternoons. The rains had turned the road to mud, and I wove my way between the puddles as he talked on about his life. Finally, the cabin appeared in my headlights, looking not so much like the cozy cabin in the woods I remembered, but a haunted house. I pulled into the gravel driveway and left the engine running. He didn't seem to notice.

"So?" he said, "What about you?"

I didn't respond.

"I've done all the talking. And you sit there saying nothing. Are you going to tell me your story or what?"

I tapped the clock on the dashboard. It was already past midnight. "I'd love . . . to visit," I whispered, "but it's late. Why don't . . . I give you . . . a call . . ."

Disappointment spread across his face. He shook his head. "Call me? Why would you? I don't even have a phone! You haven't called me in eighteen years!" He opened the door and stepped out into the rain, muttering.

"I see how it is. I take you on as my student, try to teach you what I know about storytelling, put up with your naïveté, and what do I ask in return? Money? Acknowledgment? No, nothing. Then comes the day when I ask you to tell me a story—

one story—and what do I get?" He screwed up his face, put his hands around his neck, and imitated my hoarse whisper. "We'll . . . do . . . lunch . . ." Shaking his head, he slammed the car door shut and stomped through the rain to his cabin. As he stepped onto the porch and entered the house, I sighed in relief. Angry as I was, there was something else—a twinge of sadness. Meeting him that evening had tarnished a picture that I'd long carried in my mind, of a once great storyteller who had wrestled with his own darkness. Clearly, the darkness had won out. Now I would remember him as a pathetic old man, blathering in the rain. I waited a moment, then pulled out and drove back to the highway, sure I would not see him again.

But as I neared the highway, I found myself starting to fidget, feeling unsettled. It felt wrong to leave things this way. Just before the on ramp, I turned the car around. By the time I pulled back into the driveway, the cabin was dark. I walked through the mud to the porch and stood there for several minutes, hearing nothing. I had just decided to leave when I heard Lenny's voice call from inside.

"It's open."

I entered and saw him crouched before the potbellied stove, lighting an empty egg carton, which flared up. He didn't seem at all surprised that I'd come back. "Have a seat," he said, without looking up. There were two large armchairs facing the stove, just as there had always been. I took the closer one, which had stuffing coming out of one arm. My eyes scanned the room as best they could, the only light other than the fire coming from a kerosene lantern on the kitchen table. His cabin had always been cramped, filled with books stacked on every available surface. Now, those piles had grown, and I could see their shadows on the slate floor, swaying in the light from the stove. There were also stacks of old newspapers, boxes, and an old yellow suitcase. Dust was everywhere, and its dry smell filled the room as the fire caught.

Lenny said nothing as he goaded the fire with a poker. Finally he got up and went to the kitchen. A minute later he came back with a can of mixed nuts and two glasses of water. I stared at the can, which looked like it might have a spring-loaded snake inside, and then at the glasses of water. Mine was a normal drinking glass, but his was a very delicate pink wineglass, with lines swirling up the sides.

"My grandmother's," he explained, when he saw me looking at it. "Beautiful, isn't it? She brought it all the way from Poland. There used to be four, but this is the only one left."

He sat down across from me and helped himself to a handful of nuts. I watched him for a time, still angry for the way he'd humiliated me at the bar mitzvah. Angry as I was, my pity won out. I wanted to help him.

"Well, aren't you going to say anything?" he finally said. "Or are you going to sit there and stare at me?"

"How can . . . I help . . . you?"

"I already told you. I want to hear your story."

"My story?"

"What else?" he sounded impatient. "Look, Joel, I can tell from your face that you've been through hell. I have no idea what's happened to you, but from the looks of it, someone has reached down your throat and yanked out your soul. You're a mess! But," he added, looking me up and down, "that's a great-looking suit."

The reference took me a moment to get; I had told him my father's joke years before, and it touched me that he remembered it. I felt suddenly overwhelmed. I looked into the fire for a time, then looked back up to see him sitting there, wide-eyed, waiting.

"It's a . . . long story."

"Good," he said, grabbing another handful of nuts. "That's how I like them."

"I don't know . . . where to begin."

"Doesn't matter. Wherever you start, that's the beginning. Keep on going and the ending will find you."

I sat there, groping for words to describe the pictures that sprang into my mind. Finally I gave up and began to whisper whatever came to mind. "Lost my voice," I began.

"So it seems. Go on."

In two- and three-word phrases, I explained all that I could. It wasn't easy. The words stung my throat and left me gasping for breath, but it felt good to say them just the same. Once I began I couldn't stop, the story all coming out at once. I rambled on, stopping every few words to catch my breath, until I got to that evening's bar mitzvah. "And that . . . you saw."

The look on Lenny's face was not one I expected; he was clearly shaken by my tale. When he saw me staring at him, he turned aside quickly, reaching his arm under the right side of his chair, and fished around until he came up with a wooden cigar box. He peered in the box for some time before choosing a cigar and biting off the end, which he spit into the potbellied stove. At last he lit it, took a few puffs, then settled back in his chair.

"Alright," he said, with a wave of his hand. "Go on."

I shrugged. There was nothing more to say.

His cigar hand motioned me onward. "Go on. I'm listening."

"What?"

"You've got my attention. Now what?"

"That's it."

He shook his head. "No, it's not. The story's not over. There's more."

I shrugged again and drank from my glass of water.

"C'mon, what's the point?" He waited. "Every story has a

point, a message, a moral. Otherwise there's no reason to tell it. So, what's the point?"

"No point."

"Sure there's a point. There has to be."

I shifted in my chair.

"Here's a point for you. Life has kicked you in the butt." He blew a wobbly smoke ring. "It had to happen, didn't it?" He used the cigar to point to the door. "When you walked out of that door so long ago, I knew you'd be back. And here you are, with your head down and your tail between your legs."

I stared at him, too stunned to respond. Then I slammed down the glass of water and stood to leave.

"What, running away again?" he called out, as I made my way to the door. "You don't like the truth?"

"I don't . . . like you!"

"Maybe not," he shrugged, "but you *need* me."

"Bullshit," I tried to shout as I opened the door, but got only a honk.

"Yes, you do," he said, ignoring me. "Because without me, you will become me."

I looked back through the doorway to see him standing, his face flushed. His words felt like a curse, yet another one atop the pile of curses that had built up over the past months. It was just as I stepped onto the porch that I heard him shout out a single word.

"ONCE!"

I waited. He said it again, more quietly.

"Once." And then, a third time, whispering. "Once . . . upon . . . a . . . time." There was a long pause. "On the edge of a forest, there was a palace."

I waited. "It was a magnificent palace. Inside this palace lived a prince. He had a happy life, this prince, but he was told, from the time he was a child, that whatever he did, he must not go into the forest, for it was enchanted. 'If you go in, you will be lost,' his parents had said, 'and we won't be able to come find you.' And so it was, his whole life he had done just that, and stayed out of the forest."

I found myself pulled through the doorway and into the story. "One sunny day, as he walked near the forest, the prince's curiosity overcame him. What harm could there be to peek inside? Even from the edge he could hear strange and wonderful sounds and see birds with magnificent plumage. He walked a few steps in to see trees laden with fruits he'd never seen before, alongside bubbling streams. He found himself drawn deeper into the forest until, after several hours, it was time to return. Only then did he realize he had become hopelessly lost. Frantically, he went from one path to another, trying to retrace his steps, with no luck. That night he slept in the forest, alone and afraid. The next day he resumed his wandering, desperately looking for some way out. He searched all that day, and the following day as well, but could not find it. By the end of the third day, he reached the point of despair. Just as he was on the verge of losing all hope, he spied a very old man.

"'Thank God I've found you,' said the prince, running to him. 'I can't find my way out. I've been lost in these woods for three days!'

"'Three days?' laughed the old man. 'I've been lost here for three years!'

"The prince's hopes fell. 'Then you're no use to me,' he said.

"'Ah,' said the old man. 'That is where you're wrong. For though I do not know which path leads out of these woods, I know a hundred paths that do not. Come, together we will find our way.'"

I found myself sitting, once again, across from Lenny.

"You told me *what* happened," he said quietly. "But you didn't tell me *why*."

"I . . . don't . . . know why."

"No, you don't. And without a reason you don't have a story. Just more misery. Misery without meaning. Raw suffering—of that, I've had enough. More than enough. The world is filled with it, and if I ever run out, I just read a newspaper."

"But . . . you know . . . why?"

He shrugged, thinking. "Here's what I know: Life is a tough

teacher. First she gives the test. Then she gives the lesson." He leaned toward me, speaking softly. "Look, Joel. I'm sorry. I really am. I can see that you've been through hell. And I don't have an answer, just another question. That is, are you ready to learn from what you've been through?"

I thought for a time, then nodded.

"Well that's a damn good thing. Because, until now, you've been like the guy in the monastery," he said with a smile. I didn't catch the reference, and waited. "You've done nothing but bitch and moan since you got here."

He snubbed out the cigar. Getting up from his chair, he went to a closet and came back with a blanket. "I'm exhausted," he said, motioning me toward the couch. "Why don't you sleep here tonight? We'll talk in the morning." Then he walked into his room and shut the door.

It was only then that I remembered where I was and when it was. I turned on the cell phone—which blinked with a half-dozen messages—and called Taly, who answered, groggy and furious, but relieved to know that I wasn't lying somewhere dead on the side of a road. I told her I'd be back the next day.

After I hung up, I took a long look around the room—at the books, the flickering fire, and the table, at my half-empty glass and Lenny's pink wineglass across from it.

• • •

I LAY AWAKE on Lenny's couch with springs sticking up into my back. I twisted and turned for some time before I finally found a workable position. Then, just as I reached the edge of sleep, I heard a loud growling sound. I sat up, a shot of terror running through me, until I realized it was Lenny, in the next room, snoring.

Unable to sleep, I thought about Lenny and how strange it was to find myself back in his cabin. And what of his question: Was there some reason for what I had been going through? It was a beguiling question, one I'd asked myself for months, with no answer. Yet hearing him made me wonder. He seemed convinced that somewhere there was a reason, an explanation that would make it all make sense.

Is that the way it works? For everything that happens in life, there's a reason? Even as I posed the question, I began to generate a list of things that couldn't possibly have a reason — mass slaughter of humans; horrible, random diseases; cruel accidents. The list grew fast. Yet the longer it grew, the more I wanted to believe.

The rain had stopped, and now I heard only occasional drips from the trees onto the roof of the house. Lenny's snoring had stopped as well, and I could hear birds singing. I looked outside the window to see a patch of sky through the trees, glowing a shade of purple I had never seen before.

"BREAKFAST IS SERVED."

I heard a dull thud just in front of me. I opened my eyes. There before me was a shiny bagel on the table, just a few inches from my nose. I closed my eyes.

"My friend, it comes down to this. Either this is life's way of saying 'screw you!' or maybe—" He paused for a very long time, and I opened my eyes to see beyond the bagel, where he stood. As he came into focus, he looked even worse than the night before, his pale, puffy body in only a tank top and striped boxer shorts, with legs so bruised and skinny that I wondered how they could hold him up.

"—just maybe," he finally went on, "you have been given the gift of a lifetime."

"What?" I managed.

"Could it be," he said, "that losing your voice is the best thing that's ever happened to you?"

I stared at him, more speechless than usual. A gift? What was he talking about? I had no idea what time it was, but it was too early. I pulled myself upright and stared at the bagel. In that same way that lines from songs sometimes pop into my head for no good reason, I could think of nothing more than a favorite expression of my mother's: "A bagel is a doughnut that's been to college." I reached for it. It was cold. I took a bite. The inside was frozen.

"Do you see?" he asked.

My head ached and there was a sharp twinge in my lower back where I must have slept on a spring. Beside the bagel was a mug of coffee, freeze dried from the looks of it, with brown flakes floating on the top.

"Why," he said again. "You want to know why all this is happening to you, right?"

I nodded.

"Well," he said, "it's obvious." I waited for him to go on, and when he saw he had my attention, he stopped. "Or at least it will be, when you're ready. But you're not there yet."

"What do . . . you mean?"

"Because it's the truth, and you're afraid of the truth."

I sat there for a time, chewing on the bagel and wondering what the hell he was talking about.

"The truth," he said again. "The whole truth, the real truth, and nothing but the truth, with a capital T. The truth shall set you free." He sounded like a revivalist preacher. "That's why we tell stories, don't you see? What is a story, but a golden lie that speaks the truth."

I couldn't answer.

"At least they're supposed to be. But you, you've been running from the truth. Now you have to turn around and run the other way. Chase after it! Look for it in dark places where you don't want to go." He paused, finally, and I thought he was finished. But a moment later, a grin appeared on his face.

"Tell me," he said, "have I ever told you the story of the search for truth?"

STORY ORIGIN: INDIA

The Search for Truth

There once lived a man who set off to look for truth. He scoured the world in search of it, giving up his possessions, his family, his home, all to search for truth.

After many years of wandering, his travels took him to India, where he heard tales of a distant mountain. Atop that mountain, people told him, he would find that place where truth resides.

For many months he searched, until he found the mountain of which they spoke. He climbed for several days until he finally came to the mouth of a cave. He called into it and, a minute later, his call was answered by the voice of an old woman.

"What do you want?"

"I seek the truth."

"Well, you have found me."

He entered the cave and there, in the back, saw the most horrific creature he had ever laid eyes on, huddled over a fire. Her eyes bulged out, one further than the other, and bumps covered her face. Stray teeth stuck from her mouth, and her long tangled hair hung down in matted strands.

"You?" he said. "You are truth?"

She nodded.

Though shocked at her appearance, he stayed with her and found that she was, indeed, truth. He lived there many years, learning her ways. Finally, as he prepared to leave, he asked how he could ever repay her for all she had done for him.

"I would ask simply this," she said. "When you go out in the world and speak of me, tell them I am young and beautiful!"

CHAPTER FIVE

The Search for Truth

THERE ARE SOME STORIES that make you feel warm and good inside, leaving you with the sense that all is right with the world. There are others that simply make you laugh. And then there are those you just don't know what to do with, the kind that pass through your psyche like a mouse moving through a snake. That's how it was with "The Search for Truth." I didn't know what to make of it. I didn't know what to make of Lenny. In fact, that morning as I drove up the coast from Santa Cruz toward Berkeley, I didn't know what to make of anything.

That's why I decided to drive back on Highway 1, the ribbon of road that runs along California's coast, winding its way between the sheer cliffs to the east and the tumultuous Pacific to the west. It's a longer route than the one I'd taken the night before, but strikingly beautiful, and the perfect place to be completely baffled.

I'd driven this stretch of road many times, but never tired of it. Though it was not raining that morning, I could feel a storm coming as I drove into gusts of wind so strong that they lifted up my windshield wipers, then let them whack back against the glass. In a cliff above me I spotted a lone Yucca plant, clinging on for dear life, and just above it a hummingbird, diving, swooping back up, and diving again.

I thought of all the other times I'd driven that road and remembered a favorite piece of music that I'd always saved for that particular drive — Keith Jarrett's "The Köln Concert." I fished around in my box of tapes and, sure enough, there it was, label peeling off, but the very same. I slid it into my tape deck and heard those marvelous first chords on the piano.

Keith had not aged well — at some point the tape must have gotten wet. Parts of the concert were way too loud, while others were inaudible. I let it play, though, as I drove over bridges that arched above the ocean, with the rolling clouds above and the churning waves below.

I thought again of Lenny's story, how he'd laughed when he told it, then showed me to the door, as though inviting me to leave. "Tell them I am young and beautiful." He'd said the line twice. What was that supposed to mean? That truth herself is a liar? Or that she really was beautiful? That Lenny was young and beautiful?

I was so absorbed in this question that it took me some time to notice that Keith had gone completely silent, save for a slight squeaking sound that might have been a mouse. I glanced down to see a mess of brown ribbon spewing forth from the dashboard. My tape player had chewed up Keith and spit him out.

At any other point in my life, this would have upset me, but I had run out of room to be upset. Instead I watched the tape flow down, billowing into a pile at my feet. Lenny, a sleepless night, the bar mitzvah, the past months, the droning echoes of my own voice bouncing off the inside of my head — there was no room for any more. My brain was full.

I pulled over and got out of my car, the sea air filling my lungs. Far below me, the waves crashed against the rocks, sending up a spray that felt good on my face. There was nothing to do but take it in. I'd had no great epiphany. But something had shifted inside me; I had crossed the line from confusion to bewilderment. It's a nice feeling, bewilderment — the same confusion on the inside, but wrapped in a sense of wonder.

I crossed the road and walked down a path that led to tide pools between the waves and the cliff, with seagulls circling high above. I noticed a dark spot, about twenty feet up the face of the cliff, with ice plants hanging stubbornly in front of it. I climbed up the rocks to find the entrance to a cave, larger than it had seemed from below, just tall enough for me to walk in upright. It led back a ways, then curved to the right. As it did, the sound from the wind and the ocean faded, and a few more steps took me into complete silence. At the back there was a dry spot, and even an outcropping of rock, like a bench against a wall. I sat down. This was exactly what I was looking for.

"Alright," I said to myself. "I'm ready."

For what, I had no idea. But it seemed that I had been drawn to this place. After all, wonderful things happen in caves. The man in the story had gone into a cave looking for truth, and found it. People hide in caves. I thought of a Bible story I had heard as a child about David. He was running from the soldiers of King Saul, who had been ordered to kill him. His path took him to Ein Gedi, the lavish oasis near the shores of the Dead Sea. Running for his life, he ducked into a cave—barely deep enough to hide him, but it was all he could find. As he lay there, pressed into the shadows, he saw a tiny spider at the mouth of the cave. For a moment, he forgot about the soldiers, and watched the spider as it spun its web over the mouth. Several minutes later, when the king's soldiers came by, David pressed himself against the wall and held his breath as he heard them talking outside the cave.

"He must be in here! Have you looked yet?"

"Don't bother. He's not there. Look—there's a spider web over the opening—he would have broken it if he'd gone in."

The soldiers went on, and David sat in total silence. It was then that he heard it—a very still, small voice. It was the voice of God—not the booming voice that comes when lightning strikes and the clouds part—the one that can only be heard in silence. The voice promised that God would always be with him. Throughout his life, it was this voice that guided him, inspired the Psalms he wrote, and aided him when he was lost.

I wanted to hear that voice. That still, quiet voice. I wanted it to tell me the message I'd been missing, the one that Lenny had said was so obvious. A single word of truth. Anything. Even a "hello."

Okay, I thought again. *I'm ready.*

I could feel my ears straining. I locked my teeth and sat absolutely still. Somewhere, deep in the cave, I heard a drop of water. Then silence again. Soon there were voices in my head, the usual ones, commenting and criticizing, and I shushed them away, lest they trample the still, small voice I desperately wanted to hear.

I sat there for a long time. I could feel my heart beating. From time to time I heard another drop of water, but other than that, silence.

No little voice came to me in that cave. I walked outside into the light, which seemed blindingly bright, and as I made my way back to the car, rain began to fall.

• • •

I ARRIVED HOME, expecting Taly to be furious with me — she had every right to be, after I'd left her wondering where I was until after midnight the night before. I found her on the treadmill, walking very fast. She didn't stop walking as she gave me the lecture — a vivid description of her panic, with details of the images that had run through her mind, including the muddy water flowing around my body in a ditch.

And then, after the lecture came the sigh. It was a long, slow sigh, with a shaking of her head.

"Joel," she finally said. "As I was lying in bed last night, waiting, I realized something. For months I've been hoping against hope that your voice would come back. But I can't do it anymore." She pressed the pause button and the treadmill stopped. "I love you, the kids love you, but it's time for us to go on. Without your voice."

TALY'S MESSAGE WAS NOT the one I wanted to hear. No, what I wanted to hear was that still, small voice, and I wasn't about to give up hope. I went through my days looking for signs. I got my hair cut and listened to the barber's chatter — maybe he was the messenger? I looked for messages in the clouds and omens in the shadows. I bought lottery tickets once a week, figuring I'd had enough bad luck, and I might have some good luck coming. I opened the newspaper at random, closing my eyes and pointing to a word, hoping a lightbulb would go on.

I wore my lucky sweatshirt. Everywhere I went, I looked for omens. Hummingbirds, like the one I'd seen on Highway 1, had always been my talisman, and whenever I spotted one, I took it as a good sign.

Then one night about a week later, I simply got tired of waiting. Taly and the kids were asleep and I felt like I would break in two if I didn't do something, anything. Entering the kitchen I saw a huge pile of dishes. That was something I could do, even if I didn't like to do it. I set to work, starting with the easiest items — glasses and plates — then worked my way to the more challenging pots and pans. I filled the sink with soapy water and thought again about my visit with Lenny.

The truth. He'd said I was running away from the truth. I should turn and face it. Alright, then, just what was this truth that was supposed to be so young and beautiful, I asked myself as I scraped something black from a baking pan. Well, the truth was that my voice was gone. Taly was right. The nerve that had controlled my vocal cord was not in shock; it was dead. It had been nearly four months since the surgery. It wasn't coming back. The window of opportunity had closed.

That was the truth, plain and simple, and it was far from beautiful. I scoured a frying pan which, as far as I could recall, had never been completely clean. Without my voice, my story-telling days were over. There was no other way around it. It was almost funny; I had made a career out of spinning whatever life sent me into a story, like a juggler spinning plates on sticks. But now that I had stopped, everything had come crashing down, landing here, in this sink full of dishes. Without my voice, I could no more spin stories than the miller's daughter in "Rumpelstiltskin" could spin straw into gold.

Traveling the world telling stories had been a dream, one that I'd followed for nearly twenty years. It had taken me a long way, but now it was over, gone the way of my father's violin playing and my mother's journalism. I had once read that middle age is when you stop worrying about being like your parents and discover that you've actually become them. It was at that moment, over the sink, that I turned middle aged.

I cleaned Taly's yellow teapot, which really didn't need cleaning, and remembered my high-school graduation. The valedictorian had stood before our class, eyes full of tears, and said, "These have been the best years of our lives."

"God forbid," I had said at the time. The idea that life would go downhill from high school was a horrible thought. She'd been wrong; life had gotten much better since then. Yet now, it seemed, I was on my way down. No longer was I the great dad I had once dreamed of being, or even a very good one. I was grumpy most of the time, and impatient, not unlike my own father when he was sick. I felt filthy with guilt and began to scrub the metal burner pans on the stove.

It wasn't just the kids I'd let down; it was Taly. I thought back to our wedding. It had been a traditional Jewish ceremony, and at the end the rabbi had wrapped a wineglass in a napkin, saying, "Let this remind you to treat each other well." He had placed it on the ground. "For in life, some things are fragile, like this glass. As you break it, let it remind you that there are things that, when broken, can never be repaired." I had stomped on the glass, and everyone had shouted "Mazel Tov!" And now, here we were, not quite ten years later, our glass shattered.

That was the truth, plain and simple, I had worked so hard not to see. And there was nothing beautiful about it. In fact, it was old and ugly, and the more I looked at it the uglier it got.

But here's what I did find—the longer I sat with the truth, the cleaner the dishes got. I turned the water as hot as I could stand it and remembered a Zen story I had read several times but never quite understood. A student visits a great Zen master, seeking enlightenment. The student knows he must let the master speak first, according to tradition, but the master does not speak. They sit in silence for a long time. Eventually, the master offers him a bowl of rice, and they eat in silence. Finally, the master speaks.

"Have you finished eating?" he asks.

"Yes," says the student.

"Now wash your bowl."

That's the story. I'd always found the story unsatisfying, but now, as I scoured the drip pans from the stove, it made perfect sense. Sometimes there's nothing else to do but wash the dishes.

Simple as that. We look for bells and whistles, flash and fanfare, but when you get right down to the truth, sometimes it's very simple.

Years earlier I'd traveled through Alaska, telling stories, and was amazed when I visited a glacier. I'd never known what glaciers really were — vast, frozen rivers that scrape bare everything in their path, right down to the hardest stone. That's what truth is, the stone beneath the ice.

There was something more in the Zen story: a sense of completion. He's finished, now he must wash his bowl. That's what I needed — completion. Closure. To be finished.

"Your hat?" said Lenny, when I handed it to him. It took a moment for the look of recognition to come over his face. "It's the one I gave you. And you're giving it back? Why?"

I sighed. "I'm done . . ."

It was a late Saturday morning in November, and the air was cold and crisp. I stood on the porch, watching my breath, waiting for his response.

He looked closely at the hat, which had faded over the years from charcoal gray to the color of ashes, with a shadow of darkness visible where the ribbon had come loose. Inside, the leather band had worn away, and the silk was tattered. He turned it over, holding it as though weighing it, then motioned me in.

I took my place in the overstuffed chair before the stove and told him what had happened in the weeks since I'd seen him, about the cave and the dishes. When I finished he examined the hat again.

"So, you're giving it back, right?"

I nodded.

"You're sure?" He held it out to me, but I didn't take it.

"Okay. Now what?"

I didn't know. I already missed the hat. It had been with me on so many journeys; it felt like an old friend. I made a slight move for it, but Lenny pulled away.

"Nothing weighs more than a lie," he said. "And you've been carrying this one around for some time." I nodded. "And you've finally accepted that your days of telling stories are over, right?" Though I'd said the same thing to myself, it hurt all over again to hear the words from him. "Time to move on, right?"

I nodded again.

"Good," he said. "Now, you're ready to begin."

"What?"

"Telling stories." The words made no sense, but his face was straight.

"But . . ."

"But what?"

"I can't . . . talk."

"I know," he said. "But telling stories is not about the words you say. When you have a story inside you, and an open heart, you become a conduit—the story flows through you. As for the words—" he waved a hand dismissively, "they're merely commentary."

I stared at him. He made no sense. "That's . . . ridiculous," I finally managed.

"Alright," he said. Without another word, he got up and walked to the kitchen.

I sat there waiting for several minutes, not sure whether to stay or leave. Was that it? He was through for the day? I listened for a sound from the kitchen, but heard nothing. I had just decided to leave when he called out from the kitchen.

"Because your confusion is all that you've got," he said, as though answering a question I hadn't asked. He emerged a moment later holding a tray with a blue-and-white Chinese teapot, a cup, and a saucer. It also held his pink wineglass, filled with water. He placed the glass on the table in front of his seat and set the cup and saucer on the table in front of me. Without speaking, he began to pour my tea, which was dark and brown, very slowly and deliberately. I noticed a slight palsy in his hand as he filled the cup up to the brim. But he didn't stop pouring. It flowed right over the top and onto the saucer.

I waved my hands, pointing at the cup, but he didn't stop.

The tea flowed over the saucer and onto the table, then down onto the stone floor.

"Lenny!" I tried to shout, but my voice cracked and faded.

Still pouring he said, "How can you learn when your head is already full?"

Finally I understood. It was another story, one he'd told me years before, about a Western philosopher visiting a Zen master, asking him to explain Zen. The master had responded to him just as Lenny had to me.

"I told you the day we met," Lenny went on, not the least concerned about the puddle of tea that flowed across the floor, "not to waste your time looking for answers." He put down the teapot and relit his cigar, which had gone out.

"What I've learned is that the answers come when they're ready. The harder the question, the simpler the answer. For your question, it probably comes down to a single word.

"But there's no point in guessing. The word by itself would be meaningless. First you must learn to love the question: 'Why did you lose your voice?'" He smiled. "Think of it as . . . a riddle."

Lenny had always had a thing for riddles, which he called "naked stories," and would chew on them the way a dog will chew on an old shoe. "At the heart of every story," he'd say, "you'll find a riddle." I remembered how he would spring them on me during my visits, strange riddles that made no sense. "What's green, hangs on the wall, and whistles?" he'd once asked. I'd pondered the question for some time, then finally gave up.

"You give up?" he said. "It's a herring."

"But a herring isn't green."

"So, you could paint it green."

"And a herring doesn't hang on the wall."

"You could nail it up."

"But a herring doesn't whistle."

"Ah!" he said, triumphantly. "That, I added to make it difficult."

The riddles were absurd, but I'd always laughed. Now, here he was again, talking riddles, as though they were filled with meaning.

"That's the way it works," he said, swirling the water around in his wineglass. "Usually, the answer is right there, in front of your face, so obvious you can't see it. And you never will, until you're up to your neck in the question." He blew out a puff of smoke. "But until that day, you're just sifting through sand."

"Sand?" I was lost.

He nodded. "Like the border guard. Do you know the story?"

The Border Guard

There was once a Swiss guard who worked at the border of Austria. He had worked there for many years and took a great deal of pride in his work.

One morning an Austrian man arrived at the border, riding a bicycle. On the front of the bike was a basket filled with sand. Another guard might have simply waved him through, but the Swiss guard did not. Instead, he brought out a special comb he kept for just such a purpose and began to sift through the sand in the basket. You see, he suspected the Austrian might be a smuggler. Finding nothing but sand, however, he waved the man through.

The same thing happened the next day, and the day after that. Though he never found anything, he kept on looking, day after day, for thirty years. Finally, one day, the Swiss guard spoke to the Austrian man. "I must ask you a question," he said, "that has been on my mind many years. This is my last day of work. Today I shall retire. And all these years, I suspect you have been a smuggler. Now I ask you, for I must know—are you indeed a smuggler?"

The Austrian man hesitated, and the Swiss guard reassured him. "Do not worry—I give you my word of honor that I will not prosecute you. But I must know."

"'Very well," said the Austrian. "Then I will tell you—I am indeed a smuggler."

"Ah-ha!" said the guard. "I knew it! But each day I look through your basket and find nothing but sand. Tell me, please, what have you been smuggling?"

"Bicycles."

Chapter Six

The Border Guard

"It's the hardest thing to do," Lenny said, pacing and waving his cigar. "See what's right in front of your face. God knows, I've spent most of my life looking for enlightenment on tops of mountains and now, here I am, right back where I started. The whole thing is a circle." To underscore this point, he tried to blow a smoke ring, which failed.

"Tell me," he said, "do you know how Michelangelo was chosen to paint the Sistine Chapel?" I had no idea. "He won a contest. The Pope had decided that the ceiling of the chapel must be painted by the greatest artist alive. Remember, this was during the Renaissance, and there were plenty of great artists around—Botticelli, Donatello, Leonardo. He sent bishops around Italy to collect one sample showing the very best work of each artist. Finally they got to the famous Michelangelo. He could have given them any one of his works of art, all magnificent. Instead, when he heard what they wanted, he took out a large, blank canvas and a piece of charcoal. As they watched, he drew a large circle on the canvas and handed it to the bishops.

"They didn't know what to make of it, but they took it back to the Pope, along with the rest. He examined the artworks again and again, but kept finding himself drawn back to the circle—there was something curious about it. Finally, he could look at no other paintings, just the circle. He measured it and discovered, to his shock, that it was perfect. Absolutely perfect.

"That's what life is—a perfect circle. And it is our task to draw it, again and again, on a vast, blank canvas. There's nothing more complicated and nothing more simple. You start at one point, go around, and eventually get back to the same point." With his right index finger, he slowly traced a circle in the air.

"The hard part comes when you're in the middle. You don't know what to do, which way to go, forward or backward. It's like the guy who starts to swim across the river—he gets halfway, decides it's too far, so he swims back. But you see, in life, there's no turning back."

He opened the door to the stove, and I felt a sudden rush of heat from the fire. He picked up the poker and pushed the logs around. I thought he was going to add another log, but instead he reached over to the table, picked up the hat, and tossed it into the stove. On impulse I jerked forward to grab it, then stopped myself. Using the poker he shoved it in farther, then closed the door.

I sat transfixed, watching through the glass as the flames surrounded my hat. Slowly it began to smolder, filling the stove with a blue smoke, before the crown suddenly burst into flames.

I watched it for several minutes, then looked up at Lenny staring at the flames, his face looking as sad as I felt.

"Letting go," he said softly. "That's what life is all about. We're born with fists clenched, holding tight. Yet we die with our hands open." He reached out his right hand, palm up. "We have to get good at dying, so we do it a little each day."

We sat in silence, staring into the stove, where not a trace of the hat remained. "Tell me," he finally said, "have you ever heard the story of Cortez and the first thing he did when he reached the New World?"

Still staring at where my hat had been, I was almost too dumbfounded to respond. But I did know the story—I'd often told it.

"He burned his ships. Every single one of them," Lenny said. "And do you know why?"

I nodded, glad to know the answer to at least one question. "So his . . . men would . . . not turn . . . back."

A look I can only describe as shock came over his face. I

thought he might be having a second heart attack, but then I noticed him shaking his head. He sighed, the shock giving way to disappointment.

"What's the . . ." I began.

"Don't do that," he finally said. "Ever."

"What . . ."

"Even if you've heard the story a thousand times, never assume you know it. And *never* tell the ending."

I nodded, though I still did not understand.

"Because you never know what that story may bring. And there's no telling what you might miss." He stared at me, and it felt as though he was searching for something inside me.

"So," he said. "You still haven't answered my question. Are you going to?"

"What?"

"Not what, *why*. Do you know *why* you want to tell stories?"

I stared at him, with no idea what he was talking about. I had said nothing about wanting to tell stories. Then it came to me. He was talking about that afternoon, nearly twenty years before, when I'd first knocked on his door. But he'd spoken as though no time had passed.

"Because without an answer, we're stuck," he said. "When you have one, come back."

• • •

AGAIN, LENNY HAD spun me around. I had come to tell him that I was finished with storytelling, only to have him say that this was the beginning. I had come to him with an answer and he had responded with yet another question, this one dredged up from the distant past.

Why *had* I wanted to tell stories? I tried to remember. It was a question I had been asked dozens of times before, by audiences, reporters, and people I met, when they learned I was a storyteller. I had a dozen stock answers, but now all of them seemed shallow and glib.

The truth was that I had been telling stories for as long as I could remember, starting with the ones I'd told my mother. There *were* other stories before those, but I had not wanted to hear them. They came from my grandmother, a large, pale woman with white hair and a look of terror on her face. Some mornings we would awake to find her lying asleep on the AstroTurf on the front porch of our house, with a plate of blintzes at her side. She looked so peaceful there, always dressed in the same dress, brown with white polka dots, covering her puffy body, glasses folded at her side. We would step over her on our way to school, careful not to wake her, because if we woke her, she would begin to scream.

"Where's your father? The gas men! You have to do something! They follow me! They throw gas at me!"

"Grandma, there are no gas men." We would say. "There's no such thing."

"They chase me! They throw gas at me!"

We'd try to reason with her. "You can't *throw* gas."

"Shah!" she would say. "Where's your father?"

Her hair had been white since the day she'd left Poland, as a teenager. Before that, it had been blonde. But something had happened to her that day, my father had said, in the Kraków train station. He did not know what it was, other than that it involved two Cossacks and a sum of money, and she had barely escaped alive. But, according to the story, she had awoken on the train the next morning and found that her hair was completely white. The hair color — and the fear — stayed with her until the day she died. Twice she had been locked up in insane asylums, in Cleveland and Chicago, and twice she had escaped, to follow my parents to California. Fearful as she was for her own life, she was terrified for my father's. She believed her food would save him. That's why she brought the blintzes; she was convinced my mother was trying to poison my father.

For me and my brothers, the poisoning idea was the strangest thing of all. Our mother wouldn't hurt anyone, ever, nor speak an unkind word, under any circumstance. The idea of her poisoning anyone was laughable, or would have been, had my grandmother not believed it. She would call us on the phone, sometimes ten or fifteen times a day. If my mother answered, my grandma would hang up, but if my brothers or I answered, she would start to scream.

"Your mother—she's a murderer! She's killing my Bobby!" She would start to cry, leaving us holding the phone, wondering what to do.

"You have to hang up," my father explained. "She's sick. Just hang up. And whatever you do, don't tell her what's happening in our house or where I'm working."

Each time my father got a new job, my grandmother would find out where he worked. Then she would call his boss and tell him about the poisoning and the gas men. She would do this day after day, until finally, they fired him.

She wasn't always crazy. There were times when she could be lucid and sweet, even grandmotherly. Then there would be no talk of gas men, and she would have us over to her apartment, where we would sit on her blue velvet couch eating her homemade blintzes with sour cream and strawberry jam. I wanted to love my grandmother and tried not to think of the craziness, but only of the blintzes, which I looked forward to as a special treat. Then, one night, we went to her apartment, and when she brought out the blintzes, something seemed wrong. My father sniffed at them, cut one open, and began to yell.

"Mom, what the hell are you doing?" He was furious. "Mothballs!

You put mothballs inside the blintzes! Are you trying to kill us?"
She said nothing, but stood there, shaking in fear. We never ate
blintzes there again.

These, then, were the first stories I heard—ravings of gas
men, poisonings, and death, tales tainted by madness and mothballs.

STORY ORIGIN: IRAQ

The Appointment

Once, in Baghdad, there lived a merchant who sent his servant to the marketplace to buy supplies. While there, the servant looked up, only to see Death staring at him, pointing.

In fear, the servant dashed back to his master's house.

"Master!" he begged. "You must save me! Just now, in the marketplace, I saw Death, staring at me! What can I do?"

The master thought quickly.

"Take my horse and ride as quickly as you can to the city of Samarra. You will arrive by nightfall, and there you may hide, so Death will not find you."

The servant did as he was told, and the master went off to the marketplace to confront Death.

"What is the meaning of this?" asked the merchant, when he found Death. "Why did you scare my servant so?"

"I did not mean to scare him," Death replied. "But, truth to tell, it was he who shocked me. I was astonished to see him here, in Baghdad, when I knew we had an appointment for this evening, in Samarra."

CHAPTER SEVEN

The Appointment

"THE TWO STORIES ARE THE SAME," said Lenny when he came to the ending. "And it sounds to me like you have an appointment with your grandmother."

It was a sunny day and we had walked through the woods near his cabin, down to a stream nearby. He walked slowly, on account of his limp, leaning heavily on a walking stick. I had told him of my grandmother and the gas men, of the stories I had tried to chase away. My story seemed to upset him, and he had answered it with the tale of death and talk of demons. "Death will get you in the end, and until it does, you're destined to be chased by demons. They'll find you, no matter where you go, no matter what you do. Once they get their claws in you they won't let go, until you turn around and face them. In fact, that's why Cortez burned his ships—have you heard the story?"

I wasn't about to say yes.

Lenny went on. "Well, they say that the first thing Cortez did when he got to the New World was to burn his ships, every last one of them. And do you know why?"

I shook my head.

"I'll tell you why. So that he and his men would have no choice but to face the demons!" His face broke into a broad grin, and his eyes opened wide. "Demons!" he said again, his fingers clenched like claws. "They haunt us, mocking us as we struggle through life. They chase us, and the faster we run, the harder they laugh!"

He hunched over and screwed up his face, walking toward me as he screamed in a nasal whine. "'You're useless!' they say. 'Worthless! A storyteller who can't even talk!'" He turned aside, his eyes open wide, and screamed at the top of his lungs. "'You're unfit for human contact! People can't stand you—that's why you live here in the woods, all alone!'"

He stopped suddenly, and we could both hear the echo of the final word. He looked around, trying to get his bearings. I could see he was embarrassed, and I looked away, toward the stream. When I finally looked back, I realized how frail he looked. He said nothing, but motioned in the direction of the cabin, and we walked back in silence.

"I KNOW HOW IT's supposed to work," he said later, as we sat on the steps before his cabin. "You turn and face the demons, then they go away. But I've never been able to do it. Because there's truth in their words. Young, beautiful truth. I *am* alone. No one comes to see me, except for you," he said. "And I suppose you only come because you have demons of your own, the same ones that haunted your parents, the very ones you thought you'd escaped."

I nodded; he was right.

"And what do yours say?"

Of all his questions, this was the easiest to answer. "Failure."

"Ah, failure," he said. "They do a good business, those demons. And failure *is* hell. But, for what it's worth, success is way over-rated."

I don't know if he meant this to be some consolation. It wasn't.

"People think that success will somehow turn into happiness. If only they get exactly what they want, they'll be happy. Then they get it and they're miserable, bellyaching like the monkeys in Morocco."

I waited for him to explain.

"When I was a kid, my family lived in Marrakesh for a year— great place for stories. There were monkeys everywhere and we wanted to catch them, but they were too fast. So this old man showed us what to do. You get a bottle and put a peanut inside. The monkey comes, sees the peanut, reaches his hand in and grabs it. But now his hand is a fist, with the peanut inside, and he can't get it out of the bottle. He's too excited to let go of the peanut, so he drags the bottle around. Then he's easy to catch.

"There you have it—success. And the world is filled with people, successful people, walking around with their hands stuck in bottles, wondering why they're not happy. That's the myth of our age—success will bring you happiness. But along comes the bluebird of happiness and what does it do? Shits on their heads. They don't know it, but what they really want is what you've got—failure."

Even from Lenny, this seemed farfetched.

"I'm serious," he said. "Failing is an art. Learn to do it well and you'll be happy as Larry." He stopped, with a grin. "Do you know Larry?"

I thought about it. The phrase "happy as Larry" was one I'd often heard when traveling through Ireland, but I had no idea who Larry was.

"Saint Lawrence, the Patron Saint of Happiness," Lenny explained. "Always smiling, always laughing. He was so damn happy that the Romans got sick of him. They tied him to a stake and left him to burn over a fire. A few minutes later they heard laughter and went back to see why. There was Larry, a big grin on his face. 'I'm done on this side,' he said. 'You'd better turn me over!'

"Tell me, have you ever known anyone like that? Always smiling, every time you see them? And are they *really* happy?"

I mulled his question over. The story of Larry had reminded me of my father, who spent his life laughing through his pain, and I knew he was far from happy. I thought of my mother, and how her smile grew bigger as things got harder. The smile came through in her voice and in all the phone messages that had been piling up, unanswered, on my machine. No matter how *fine* she said things were, I know she was not *really* happy. I was about to give up my search when I remembered someone.

"Maybe the boy . . . on the bike."

"Who's that?"

I told Lenny about Ricky. He lived on the cul-de-sac down the street from us, when I was growing up. We all called him "the boy on the bike." He was developmentally disabled— retarded, we said in those days. He always wore a red sweater and rode his bike around in circles, sometimes clockwise, sometimes counterclockwise. We passed him every time we drove to the freeway, and each time he would stop and wave at us, a huge smile on his face. I suppose he waved at everyone. We would wave back, and he would go on riding. I thought about all the times I'd seen him; he was always happy. Whether he was *really* happy, I had no idea.

"Good," said Lenny. "One smiling kid, in a red sweater, on a bike. And what made him so happy?"

I had no idea.

"Seems to me he rode around in circles, never thinking he should be doing something else or being someone else. He may not have been a genius, but it sounds like he was happier than many brilliant people, who walk around the world burdened by the ridiculous notion that their life should be different than it is. 'I should be rich,' they say. 'I should be famous.' 'I should be better looking.' Everyone has their 'shoulds'; I know a guy who walks around saying to himself, 'I should be able to talk.'"

It was getting cold, so we went inside. Lenny began to build a fire, but I motioned for him to sit, while I arranged the wood in the stove, crumbled a piece of newspaper, and lit a match.

"I'll tell you, nothing screws up life like our expectations. We like to pretend we can outsmart God, the great storyteller in the sky. So what happens? God looks down and sees some fool who thinks he's got life figured out, then sneaks up from behind and kicks him in the butt. Or, in your case, steps on his foot. Right on the big toe. Wham!"

He'd lost me again.

"Gout. That was God getting your attention. Same thing happened to me."

"Gout?"

"Nah. It happened when I was surfing." I thought I'd misheard him. Whatever Lenny was, he did not look like a surfer. "That's why I came to Santa Cruz in the first place."

"Surfing?"

"Sure. For the waves." I tried to picture him on a surfboard, but couldn't. "This was long before you ever met me, before I went to grad school or ever thought about telling stories. I hitched out here from New Jersey and spent every day riding the waves and every night partying on the boardwalk.

"Have you ever surfed?" he asked.

I shook my head.

"You should try it. There's nothing better—like flying on water." He shook his head, a sad smile on his face. "I was good, too, as good as anyone on the beach. And you know why? Because I had no fear. I *knew* that nothing could harm me. In rough weather, others guys would chicken out. But I'd go out in storms, fifteen foot swells." He paused for a time, thinking about it. "One morning, I met the most magnificent wave I'd ever seen. A rogue, it must have been twenty-five feet, perfectly formed. I got on my board, ready to ride, and you know what happened?" He paused and picked out a cigar. I waited.

"It beat the holy hell out of me. Bent me over backward, wrapped me around my board, chewed me up, and spit me out on the beach. Almost killed me. Five cracked vertebrae, two broken ribs, and this"— he reached with his right hand to pick up his left hand by the wrist—"no feeling from the elbow down."

He looked at it and laughed. "You know, I used to be left-handed?

"I went through four operations before they gave up. Not just on my hand, which was hopeless from the start, but on my back. Said my vertebrae looked like a handful of teeth. I've had shooting pains in my left leg, every day since. Even now, if I sit for more than twenty minutes my body feels like it's being whacked with a baseball bat. And you know the worst part?"

"What?"

"I had to give up surfing." He laughed. "I spent all those months in and out of hospitals, asking myself one question—Why? Why had this happened to me?" He stopped pacing and sat down in his chair. "Well, apparently, it's the same thing everyone wonders; I wonder about my accident, you wonder about your voice. And that's just the point—*everyone* wonders. So maybe we should be asking 'Why us?' instead. And the answer is, that's life. It's filled with misery and suffering and loss after loss until, in the end, you lose everything."

"Are you . . . trying to . . . cheer me up?"

"Why would I do that? I've done everything I can to chase away the unicorns and dry up the rainbows, so you can face your demons and see life for what it is: the sum total of all we've lost, divided by what we learn from it. And you'll go on suffering until you've learned your lesson. The future has slipped through your fingers, the past is gone, and you're left with nothing but this very moment, right here, right now."

"Where?"

In answer, he stood up from his chair and walked around the

cabin, his able hand motioning in a circle around him. "Looks to me like you're right in the middle of a story. *Your* story."

I shook my head, and he responded with a shrug.

"Sounds like a story to me. Think about it. You've got all the elements. The main character—you—loses something precious —your voice—and so, goes off on an adventure. In fact, there's only one difference between this story and one you would tell."

"What?"

"You can't tell it!" He beamed. "Because you can't talk! And you know where that leaves you?"

"Screwed?"

He shook his head. "Would you knock off the self-pity?" He snubbed out his cigar. "All that you're seeing, your feelings, your confusion—that's how a story looks from the inside."

"But I'm real!" I insisted.

"And *that's* what makes it a good story. It all makes sense. You walked out of my door twenty years ago and set off to seek adventure. And now, here you are, back again, in the middle of a grand adventure. What more do you want?"

"Out."

"It doesn't work that way. What would happen if a character tried to escape from a story you were telling?"

I thought about it. I had no idea. None of my characters had ever tried to escape from their stories.

"They stay put, right?" said Lenny. "Because if they didn't, they'd ruin the story. And that's your problem. For months now, you've been trying to scrape and claw your way out of your own story." He shook his head. "But that's not the way it works. You're in a story. I'm in a story. Everyone is inside a story, whether they like it or not."

His words brought to mind an old episode of *Star Trek,* where Captain Kirk and the crew came to a strange planet, filled with characters from the distant corners of their imaginations, whom they battle to within inches of their lives — before they finally figure out that the whole place is actually an intergalactic amusement park, meant for their pleasure.

"Now, tell me, what story do you think you're in?"

I thought back over the months since I'd lost my voice. "Job?" I joked.

His eyes lit up. "Maybe."

"Terrible story. Cruel."

"No, Job is a great story. Did you know that it's the only place in the whole Bible where God laughs?" I didn't. "What's more, Job is one of only two words in English that change their pronunciation when you capitalize them." Job — job. I tried to ask what the other was, but he was on to the next point. "And it has a great moral; simply put — 'there are things in this life we just don't understand.'

"Islam teaches the same lesson. In the Koran, God takes Moses to the Red Sea, where he sees a little sparrow dive down for a mouthful of water. 'You see how much water is in the sea?' asks God. 'That is how much knowledge there is. And the water the sparrow drinks? That is how much humans know.'"

I LEFT LENNY'S, thinking back to a film I had seen in high school physiology, about a man who was given a special pair of glasses that made the world appear to be upside-down and backward. Mr. Clarkson showed it to us to demonstrate how marvelously adaptive the human brain can be. As scientists strap the glasses on the man's head, a warning flashes across the screen: "DO NOT TRY THIS AT HOME!" He wears the glasses every day and night for six weeks. At first he is a wreck, falling down, bumping into things, and throwing up. Then, suddenly, after about five weeks, his brain flips the picture over, so the world appears normal. He is able to go about his daily life, ride a bicycle, drive a car, and so on. So complete is his transformation, in fact, that once the glasses are removed, the world appears to him to be upside-down and backward once again, and it takes another five weeks for him to get it straight.

Visiting Lenny was like strapping on those glasses. To hear him tell it, everything was the opposite of how it looked; right was left and up was down. All the bad things that had happened to me—they were good. The way to find the answer to a question was to stop looking, and the reason I couldn't see it was because it was right in front of my face.

Though seeing things upside down was strange, seeing them backward was scary. After visiting Lenny, I would find that my future had moved behind me and my past suddenly stood before me, getting closer all the time.

I had long ago mined my past for stories, but the ones that came to me now were the stories I had tried to forget. I could see my father again, though he was not laughing. It was a hot night and I had awoken, unable to sleep. I went to the kitchen for water but stopped when I came upon him, hunched over the Formica table, as he tried to assemble a black box, filled with electronics and held together by masking tape—the same invention he had been working on for years. I watched from the doorway as he reached to pick up a small screw, but his knobby fingers could not grasp it. He tried again and again, and once almost had it, but it slipped out, and onto the floor. This time, he put his head in his hands. I did not want to see his tears so, without a word, I slipped off back to bed.

I heard my grandmother again, the echoes of her screams, and the long strings of Yiddish curses she hurled at my mother. I tried to push her picture out of my mind, but I could not. She came back, screaming more loudly, just as frightening as she had been when I was a child. Reminding myself of Lenny's advice about demons, I stood my ground, turned to face her, and found myself staring into her dark eyes. When I turned from her, it was to see the face of my mother, frozen in fear. A moment later, I saw my mother's hand reach up to her hearing aid and switch it off. The terror drained from her face, and in its place she forced a smile. That smile was the hardest thing to watch.

AS FAR AS I CAN RECALL, the movie about the guy with the glasses showed nothing about the effect they had on his family. But I'm sure it wasn't easy for them. I know it wasn't easy for mine; they had no idea what to make of my mood swings, from sullenness to occasional euphoria and back. Nor did I know how to explain what was happening to me, because I didn't understand it myself.

Taly had begun to move on without me. Rather than obsess about her health, she had begun to do something about it, eating mindfully and exercising often. She felt great and looked great, but seemed far away; we were on parallel tracks, with her miles ahead of me. It was at night that I felt the distance. Until now, even in the midst of fights, we'd always slept like spoons; now we slept like knives, each in our own world. And I could not imagine—let alone say—words that might rebuild the bridge between us.

It seemed my whole life had become a series of magic words I could not say. Among them was that word Lenny had mentioned, the answer to a riddle I could only solve by not thinking about it. I thought about it constantly.

"Relax," Lenny would say in response to my frustration. "In

time, the muddy waters will settle. And when you look into them, do you know what you'll see?"

I waited.

"Signs and wonders, my friend. Signs and wonders."

That's just what happened several days later, on a day when Taly was at work, the kids were in school, and the rain had stopped, so there was not a sound to be heard. I sat very still in my office, trying not to think of the answer to the question, putting every thought out of my brain, trying not to think of anything at all, making my mind a pool of simple stillness. *Show me a sign.*

That's when the jackhammering began. It sounded like thunder at first, and I could feel it through the floor and see the pictures rattling on the wall. It stopped for a moment, then started again.

Some months earlier, a couple had purchased the house kitty-corner from ours, a once beautiful old building that had become home to about thirty cats. They made plans to restore the place and had been waiting for a break in the rain to start construction.

The noise became a constant source of torment, starting up at random intervals throughout the day. Just when I thought it had stopped, and I began to whisper something to Taly or the kids, it would start again, as though on cue. Sometimes, in lieu of jackhammering, I would hear the sounds of a circular saw or an electric hammer.

Not wanting to admit defeat, I tried to shout over it.

"Michaela . . . honk! Could you . . . honk!"

"What?" Michaela would say. "I can't hear you. Speak louder!"

I tried that for two weeks. And then it happened, one day, as I was asking Elijah to pass the breakfast cereal. I stopped trying to talk over the noise. In fact, I stopped trying to talk the rest of the day. And even that evening, when everyone had gone to bed and I was all alone, with no construction noise, I did not try to talk. I gave up.

Only then did I realize that I had been trying, without success, to push sound from my mouth, every waking hour of every day, ever since the operation—seven months. Though I'd known intellectually I could not speak, my body had refused to believe it, until that moment.

Suddenly, I felt free, lighter. It was like an experiment I used to do as a kid. I would stand in a doorway, arms at my sides, pushing against the doorjamb as hard as I could for thirty seconds. Then, I would step out, relax, and my arms would float toward the sky, as though tied to balloons.

That's how the silence felt. I remembered another Zen story, about two monks walking after a storm. They spot a beautiful young woman dressed in a fine kimono, standing at one side of a stream. She is unable to cross the stream, so the younger of the two monks picks her up and carries her to the other side. They go on their way, but the older monk is furious. He says nothing until he reaches the monastery, whereupon he turns to the younger monk.

"How could you do that?" he shouts. "You know we made a vow not to touch a woman!"

The younger monk smiles. "The woman in the kimono? I put her down hours ago. Why are you still carrying her?"

My voice had become a useless limb that I had dragged around for so long that I had forgotten I was carrying it. That afternoon I put it down.

The moment I did, something happened. I began to hear other people's voices in a new way. All my life, I've loved the sound of the human voice. But since that morning in the hospital, each voice I'd heard had come to me through the filter of envy; the speaker had something that I did not, and I wanted it, more than I've ever wanted anything. Now that the filter was gone, I was once again able to appreciate the bouquet of voices around me. There was Michaela's little voice, so small and sweet, and the unyielding earnestness that infused Elijah's. I heard the melody that came through Taly's voice, even when she was not singing. There was something to notice in each voice around me, from Ron the postman's slightly grainy, Midwestern drawl, to the warmth and openness that came through in every word spoken by Ginger, Michaela's preschool teacher.

All these I could suddenly hear from a distance, the way one might appreciate a ballet if one has never thought of becoming a dancer, or the artistry of a basketball player if one does not play the game. Talking was natural for them, as it had once been for me. But that door had closed and—just as in my mother's saying —a window had opened. It was the window to the world of silence, a world I had too long overlooked.

I remembered an article I'd once read about a sound technician who was traveling the world with his tape recorder, looking for the quietest places, trying to capture complete silence. At the time it had struck me as a pointless task—even if he had been completely successful, he'd have come home with a blank tape. Now, as I thought of him again, his plan seemed profound. The beauty of it lay in the fact that real silence—absolute, complete silence—does not exist. All we can do is peel back the layers of noise in this world, revealing the quieter sounds beneath. And gradually, the article said, we may hear the quietest sounds of all—the flow of an underground stream, a bug eating a leaf, or the sound made by a tiny fish as it spits a drop of water to bring down a passing insect.

Like that sound technician, I sought out silence, whenever I could. As most of my nights were spent writing, I found time during the days to go in search of the quietest places I could find, riding my bike into the hills behind Berkeley, looking for a sheltered place. Then I would sit there, my eyes closed, to see how little I could hear.

STORY ORIGIN: JEWISH, POLAND

The Wisdom of Chelm

Hidden away in the mountains of Poland, somewhere on the road from Warsaw to Chotzenplotz, is the tiny village known as Chelm. The people of Chelm are the greatest fools in the world, though they do not think of themselves as such. Rather, they consider themselves the wisest people in the world and their elders the wisest of the wise.

They spend their days in contemplation of the great questions of life, such as, "Which is more important— the sun or the moon?" A question like this can split the town for weeks, until the matter is taken up by the elders themselves, who ponder it carefully, stroking their beards and furrowing their brows. At long last, the question will finally be settled by Chaimyonkel, the very wisest of the elders, who will rule that, while the sun is indeed important, the moon is much more important, for it shines at night, when it is dark, and we most need the light.

Likewise, it was his wisdom that comforted Chelm when a tragedy struck the town—one night there was a terrible fire, and the people of Chelm fought the whole night through to extinguish the flames. In the morning, the Chelmites roundly cursed the fire except for Chaimyonkel, who disagreed.

"The fire was a blessing!" he said. "For it gave us light! And without this light, how could we have ever seen our way to put out the fire?"

Getting to Chelm is difficult, for the road is fraught with perils. In order to find it, you must first be lost. You start walking from Warsaw on a sunny day when suddenly, a storm comes up—a blizzard. Day turns to night as you struggle through the snow until you can no longer tell left from right, up from down. At that point, you make a left turn and walk until you see a man digging around in the snow, under a streetlamp.

"Did you lose something?" you ask.

"Yes, I lost my keys."

So you bend down to help him look, with no success.

"Where exactly did you lose them?" you finally ask.

"Down the street, by the temple."

"Why are you looking here?"

"The light is better."

Only then, when wisdom and foolishness trade places, do you know you have arrived in Chelm.

Chapter Eight

The Wisdom of Chelm

"Oh, I get it," Lenny said at last. "Silence."

I had been standing on his porch for what may have been five minutes, but seemed like an hour, as he asked me one question after another, waiting for me to speak. But I said nothing, nor did I try. Much as I wanted to convey what I'd learned, saying anything about it seemed pointless.

Saying nothing in response, he motioned me inside, to sit before the fire. It was only after a very long time that he spoke.

"People think storytelling is about talking; it isn't. It's about silence and giving shape to that silence. Silence is our canvas. It is the clay from which we sculpt our world, the marble at which we chip away. And how do we chip away at it? With our words! We begin a story in silence, the purer the better. And when we stop to pause"—and here he paused, for a long time—"we can see, actually feel, the shape of the silence we have created. If you've come to silence, Joel, you're halfway there."

Still, I said nothing, soaking up the rare praise.

"You know," he went on, as we sat down, "I've been thinking about just what story you're in. It's hard to say, of course, because it changes all the time—like the lines on the palms of your hands. That's because God is up there, twisting plots, adding details. And just when you think you've got it figured out, along comes a turn. At the moment, I wonder if you might be somewhere in Chelm. You know about Chelm, don't you? The Polish Jewish town of fools?"

Of course I knew. Those were the stories my mother had almost told me. I had since learned many of them and told dozens in my performances. But as he said the word "Polish," something came to me. I pulled out a pen and wrote on a scrap of paper.

"Polish—polish."

"Good," he said. "Polish, polish, Job and job. You see? Eventually, riddles solve themselves. And when they do, we must find new ones. Because if we don't, we are in danger of becoming wise, wise like the fools of Chelm, looking for what we've lost under the streetlamp because the light is better. Their foolishness lies not in what they do, but in believing they are wise."

He stared off into the distance for a long time. Finally he turned back to me.

"Have I ever told you about Pearl?"

I shook my head.

"No, I suppose I wouldn't have." He sighed. "She was 'the imperfect woman.' You must know the story." I didn't. "It's about Mullah Nasrudin."

I sat back in anticipation; I've always loved stories about the great Sufi mystic, the balding trickster-fool.

"Nasrudin was always being asked to give advice at weddings. Finally, a disciple asked why he himself had never married. 'Ah,' he explained. 'I decided I would marry only when I found the perfect woman. For many years I searched, and I encountered many a woman who was kind, beautiful, intelligent. Yet not one of them was perfect. Each one had some small flaw.

"'Then one day,' says Nasrudin, 'I saw her. I knew it instantly. There was no question in my mind. She was perfect in every regard. Sure enough, as I came to know her, I found she was, indeed, a gem without flaw.'

"'So why didn't you marry her?' asked the disciple.

"Nasrudin sighed. 'There was just one problem.'

"'You found an imperfection?'

"Nasrudin shook his head. 'No, simply this — she was looking for the perfect man.'"

Lenny shook his head. "Pearl," he sighed again, "was imperfect in all the right ways. I had looked for years to find her — didn't want to screw up again, like I did in my first marriage. A disaster. But within an hour of meeting Pearl, I knew she was the one. I could see it in her face. I could feel it in the bottom of my soul. It was meant to be. And you know what happened?"

I waited.

"We got married. She was my second wife. She was a dancer, jazz. Came here from New Zealand. She lived and breathed music. We honeymooned in Fiji and drank mango nectar under the stars." He stopped for a moment and a dreamy look washed over his face.

"We came back here, bought this cabin, set up a life together." He shook his head. "We were happy as could be. You know, you can go through life, never realizing just how lonely you are, until you fall in love." With some effort, he got out of his chair, walked to his room, and came back with a picture in a silver frame, which he handed to me. She was a bright-eyed woman with curly brown hair.

"Beautiful, isn't she?" I nodded. "But a month after we were married she was diagnosed with ovarian cancer. Five months later, she was dead. All together, I had only ten months with her." He stopped for a moment, and I could see tears. "But those ten months—they were the greatest gift I've ever been given. They got sweeter as they went along. Sweeter—not easier. They were hell. Doctors, operations, chemo, pills. She withered away, her hair fell out—she was gorgeous. And she got more beautiful, every day, until the end. I lived more in those six months than I have in all the rest of my life." He looked away for a time, then added, "You're never more alive than when you're standing next to death."

I LEFT LENNY that afternoon, marveling at how different stories can be, how some stories can make us laugh, while others make us cry. I thought about bedtime stories, which send us off to sleep, and Zen stories, which wake us up with their strange, paradoxical twists. Other stories do this as well, because they sneak up on us when we're not expecting them. Lenny's last story had opened up something inside me. I noticed it from the moment I left him; the world seemed closer. Driving home, seeing my house, the trash waiting to be taken out—nothing had really changed, but I found that I saw it more clearly. It wasn't better, it wasn't worse; it simply had the sheen of reality.

The story of Pearl had landed somewhere deep inside me, and it surfaced again and again, especially at night, over the next weeks. I found myself thinking about death—not just my father's, which I'd thought about for years, but my own, the one I'd avoided by having the tumor removed. I realized that, in all my focus on my voice and its return, I hadn't quite let in just how close I had come to dying.

One night I woke early, just before dawn, and went to check on the kids, as I often do. Elijah was sound asleep. In the glow of his night-light, I looked at him a long time, then at the flags scattered around the room. He had recently started inventing flags for made-up countries where the Beanie Babies lived, making the flags from wooden chopsticks and a white sheet Taly had cut up. These were in a basket and I sifted through them, until I found what I was looking for. It was one he had not yet colored, and I borrowed it. I sat there on the floor, cross-legged, waving it.

A minute later Michaela awoke, rubbed her eyes, and crawled out of bed. She walked over to me and sat on my lap. She didn't say a word, but merely looked at the flag, then up at me, her hands resting on my knees, and I felt like the luckiest man alive.

THE NEXT MORNING I made pancakes for the kids' breakfast — a dad activity that I'd come to love. Inside my head I heard "Oh, What a Beautiful Mornin'" from *Oklahoma!* and though I couldn't sing it, I whistled. That morning I became a short-order cook, as the kids put in their orders for pancakes.

"I want an E on mine," said Elijah.

"And I want an M," said Michaela.

As I made their pancakes, I looked up at them and felt something strange, a feeling I could not name. What was it?

"Is this an M or an E?" asked Michaela.

"It depends which way you look at it," answered Elijah. "But what's this one?"

He pointed to a huge pancake I'd made, as big as a plate, filled with holes.

Standing between them, I pulled them both close to me and whispered. "It's a map . . . of the stars."

Delight spread across their faces, and that's when it hit me. No wonder I hadn't recognized the feeling; it had been so long.

I was happy.

Buried Treasures

Long ago, in the Polish city of Kraków, there lived a poor Jewish tailor by the name of Yaakov ben Yekel. Hard as he might work, he could never seem to make enough money to feed his wife and children. With nothing else to do, he went to the temple, where he prayed for a miracle.

That very night he had a magnificent dream. In it, he found himself in the distant city of Prague—a place he had never been before. Yet now, he could see it all clearly, even feel the breeze as he walked through its streets, with a shovel on his shoulder. Finally he came to a spot on the ground. There, he began to dig a hole, and as he did so he heard a loud voice call to him, "Yaakov ben Yekel—go to Prague! There is something there for you!"

He had the same dream, again and again, each time more vivid than the time before. Finally, he realized there was nothing for him to do but go to Prague.

It took him weeks to walk there, through the rain and snow, but when he finally arrived, he was astonished by what he saw. The city of Prague appeared exactly as it had in his dream. He ran through the streets, finally coming to the very spot he had seen in his dream —and began to dig.

Suddenly, he felt a hand on his shoulder.

"What are you doing?" said an angry voice. There, beside Yaakov, stood a guard, the biggest man he had ever seen. Yaakov was terrified. Not knowing what else to say, Yaakov told the truth.

"I'm digging here . . . because I had a dream—"

"Ha!" laughed the guard. "A dream?" He slapped Yaakov's face. "You look like a dreamer, thin, weak, sickly! Dreams are for fools, like you!" said the guard. "Funny you mention dreams—last night, I had a dream. A voice spoke to me and said 'You there, Ivan, go off to the town of Kraków—and there, in the miserable little house of a tailor'—something like Yankel, or Yekel—'you will find, under his stove, a great treasure.' It was a crazy dream—but you don't see me going off to Kraków, do you? No, dreams are for fools!"

With this, the guard kicked him out of the city, and Yaakov began the long walk home. When he arrived, weeks later, he kissed and hugged his whole family—then went right to the stove. He pushed it aside and began to dig. He dug for hours but, in the end, found only dirt. Finally, exhausted, he fell asleep.

As he slept, his children played in the hole, digging deeper until his youngest daughter found something that felt like an old soup pot. With her brothers and sisters, she pulled it up and brought it to Yaakov. He pried it open and found that it was filled with old gold and silver coins—a fortune, enough money to feed his family, fix his house, and even to do what he had always wanted to do—give to the poor.

He lived a good life until, finally, as a very old man,

he found himself with but one coin left. This, he decided to give to a beggar.

"Thank you," said the beggar. "And for you, Yaakov, I have two words of advice."

"Advice?" asked Yaakov.

"Yes," said the beggar. "Dig deeper."

Yaakov returned to the stove, under which he found the same hole, and began to dig again. This time he found a box. Though it was small, he opened it to find it filled with diamonds, rubies, and emeralds—a greater treasure than he had ever imagined.

He even had enough money to build a small house of study, at a place where two roads meet. Legend has it that this building still stands today. It is a place for travelers to stop and rest, to think about where they have been and where they are going. You will know you have arrived there when you see these words, written on the wall in gold letters: "Sometimes you must follow your dreams very far to find that which is closest to your heart."

Chapter Nine

Buried Treasures

I knew something was wrong when I arrived at Lenny's cabin. It was too quiet. The sun was just setting as I knocked on the door. I heard no answer, then knocked again. Finally I pushed open the door.

In the darkness I could see the usual stacks of books, and as my eyes adjusted to the light I saw Lenny in his chair, staring into space.

"Lenny?" I called. No response.

The room still smelled of the same things — mildew, age, and cigar smoke, but there was another smell. Whiskey. There, at his feet, was a bottle of Old Crow, lying on its side. I listened for a time; his breathing was heavy and slow. I looked right into his eyes — wide open, but no one was there.

I picked up the bottle and poured the rest down the kitchen sink. The wastebasket was overflowing, so I stuffed it down, figuring I might as well take it outside.

"Lenny?" I whispered in his ear. Nothing. I had no idea what to do. I moved into his field of vision—nothing. From the look in his eyes, he was in some dark place, a trance.

I waited for ten minutes. Finally, I realized there was nothing I could do, and turned toward the door.

"Tell me something," I heard him say.

I went back to him. He hadn't moved. I watched and waited. Finally, after a long time, he turned to me and spoke again.

"Tell me something," he said again. His voice sounded far away. "When does the night end?" There was a long pause, during which time he seemed to be chewing something. "That is the question asked of the rabbi by his disciples." His voice sounded mournful, almost pleading. He turned to stare at me, but his eyes did not seem to focus.

"'Does it end when you can see the morning star?' asked one.

"'No,' said the rabbi. 'That is not the time.'

"'Is it when you can see all the lines on the palm of your hand?' asked another.

"'No, that is still not the time,' said the rabbi.

"'Then when?' asked the disciples.

"'When you can look at your neighbor's face and see that it is your own. Then, at last, the long night is over.'"

OVER THE NEXT several days I wondered what, if anything, I might do to help Lenny. Though I'd had no direct experience with the matter, I knew that stopping an alcoholic who had started drinking again was like fighting with the wind. I had trouble enough dealing with him sober, but drunk? What could I do?

It wasn't just worry I felt, but guilt as well. I remembered a story I'd heard from a friend of mine who had worked in Micronesia for a time, on the island of Pohnpei. The people there swore it was true. There was a boy who was a gifted runner, the fastest in his school. But he was in a horrible auto accident, which left him a paraplegic; the doctors said he would never have use of his legs again.

One day as he lay in the hospital, an old woman came in, her body decrepit with age. "God!" she said aloud. "It's not fair! You take his legs, so young and strong. Why not take mine instead?"

According to my friend, she never walked again, but he went on to become the greatest runner the island had ever known. I thought of that story as I wondered what to do about Lenny. It seemed something had been exchanged between us; he had taken my misery and given me the joy he'd kept hidden.

I WAS STILL TRYING to figure out what to do some days later when I got a phone call from a man who identified himself as a doctor.

"May I speak to Mr. ben Izzy?" he said. His voice was older, and gruff.

"Speaking."

There was a long pause, and I could tell he was confused. "Excuse me, I need to speak to *Mr.* ben Izzy. Is your husband home?"

I tried to muster up my deepest, loudest whisper. "I'm Mr. . . . ben Izzy."

He cleared his throat and went on. "Right. Well, I'm afraid the news is not good." Now I was confused. I hadn't seen a doctor in months. What bad news could he have to give me?

"Well, her lab tests came back and confirmed what we'd feared. I'm afraid it's cancer. Late-stage metastatic lung cancer."

"Who?"

"Why, your mother, of course. She asked us to call you as soon as we had the results of the surgery."

"Surgery?"

"This morning. You didn't know? Didn't anyone tell you?"

I waited, numb.

"I'm sorry. There must have been a mistake. A social worker was supposed to have called you." He took a deep breath. "Your mother came in to the hospital yesterday with difficulty breathing. She said she'd been bothered by a cold for over a month. We thought it might be bronchitis, but it turned out to be a collapsed lung. We took X-rays but they weren't conclusive, so this morning we operated, just exploratory surgery. To tell you the truth, though, I didn't need to see the lab results. It looks bad in there. I'm afraid she doesn't have long."

I could not believe the words I was hearing. I thought of the messages my mom had left on my answering machine. She had sounded like she had a cold. Not that she'd complained about it— she hadn't—but I could hear it in her voice as she told me how well things were going. In a daze, I wrote down the information— the hospital in Southern California, phone numbers, and so on.

"How long?" I managed to ask.

"You'd better come now."

THERE'S A ZEN STORY that has always haunted me. It tells of a master who had a very particular way of indicating he had made a point. After he finished speaking, he would raise his hand, his index finger bent ever so slightly, and say, "Ah-ha!"

This gesture was his trademark, and no other monk would think of using it. It happened, though, that one of his students, having seen this gesture many times, took to imitating it. He never did this in the presence of the master, of course, but often, in discussions with other students, when making a point, he would raise his hand, his finger up just so, and intone, "Ah-ha!"

One day the master called him before the class to answer a question. So pleased was the student with his answer that, when he finished, he boldly raised his hand, index finger up, and said, "Ah-ha!"

The class was shocked at his audacity and wondered how the master would respond. He merely asked him to repeat the answer, which he did gladly, again adding the signature, "Ah-ha!" This time, though, the teacher grabbed his wrist, pulled his hand down to the desk, removed a cleaver from behind it, and chopped off his finger. The student screamed in agony and went running from the room, blood spurting from his hand. Before he reached the door, though, the teacher called after him.

"One more thing—" said the teacher.

"What?" screamed the student.

The teacher smiled, raised his hand with his finger just so, and said, "Ah-ha!"

It was not a story I'd ever told; from the moment I heard it, I had tried not to think about it. Yet that's the story that came to me, again and again, as the plane began its descent to Los Angeles International Airport. This, then, was the way God worked. Just when you thought you understood something about life— wham! Then, a moment later, "Ah-ha!"

I tried to put the story out of my mind, along with my anger—an airplane is no place to be furious at God. Instead I tried to be mad at the flight attendants, with their smug service and cheap pretzels, but it didn't help. I was mad at me. Mad for having been so disconnected from my mother. Mad at myself for having gotten sick. And mad at my voice for not working.

Below me spread miles and miles of megalopolis. Near the

airport I could see vast parking lots, some that must have had ten thousand cars, and freeways, everywhere freeways, branching off in all directions with traffic at a Friday afternoon standstill. Through the brown air I could see the endless grids of streets, square blocks with houses, extending until they vanished into the haze. As the plane descended, I found myself doing the same thing I'd always done when I'd flown into Los Angeles—holding my breath for as long as I could.

I did not want to think about where I was going and what I had to do. Instead, I replayed the day before. After the phone call, in one of those strange coincidences that seem to occur around a death, Elijah and Michaela came running in to tell me they had found a dead bird on the porch.

"We need to bury it," said Elijah. I found a shoe box, which the kids decorated with construction paper to make it into a coffin. Elijah carefully wrote "BIRD" on the box, and Michaela decorated it with stickers of butterflies. As we buried the bird in a corner of our yard, I did my best to explain that Grandma Gladys was dying and soon they would be going to a real funeral.

Taly came home just as we were saying Kaddish for the bird. After the kids went back to playing, I told her about my mom. She was stunned at first and then started to ask questions— "Have they tried . . ." and "What about . . ."—none of which I could answer.

Later that evening, as I searched our room for clothes to

throw into my suitcase, she came in and sat on the bed. She motioned for me to do the same, but I didn't; I was too angry. So she sat there, watching me.

"So, what are you going to do?" she finally said.

I shrugged and kept on packing.

"This is important, Joel. This is what life is all about."

"It sucks," I whispered, packing the underwear I'd found and looking for socks.

"That's right. But this is life. Your life. And it's important."

"It sucks," I reiterated.

"Yes, it does. But that doesn't change anything. You have work to do."

"Sucks."

"They're in the bottom drawer, on the left." I didn't catch her meaning, so I looked, and there were a half-dozen pairs of socks, rolled up in balls. "Joel, you've been given a chance. The chance that few of us get and fewer take."

I knew what she meant. Just after we'd started dating, her own mother had died, also of lung cancer. As the end neared, Taly flew off to be with her. As soon as she arrived at the hospital, her mother turned to her and said, "We have to talk."

"Now?" asked Taly.

"Soon." Fifteen minutes later she slipped into a coma and never came out.

I could see Taly reliving the memory. "Joel," she said at last, "you have to say good-bye."

I grabbed several balls of socks from the drawer, came to her ear and whispered, "*Say* good-bye? . . . How the . . . hell am . . . I supposed . . ?"

"Joel, you don't get it. The time for self-pity is over. You need to say good-bye to your mother. And she needs to say good-bye to you."

"But how . . ."

"I don't know. But I believe in you. And when you see her, say all that you have to say. Don't wait. Because soon, it will be the last time."

LAX WAS AS CROWDED as I'd ever seen it, and as I waited in line for the rental car, I wondered what I would do when I saw my mother. I tried to picture her and remembered a photo on my mantlepiece, taken on her seventieth birthday, with her wearing her red-and-orange party dress. She looked so happy. But now that seemed so far away. I thought of the joy on her face as she had watched me perform, in so many times and so many places. How had we come to be so far apart? She had brought me into this world, I reminded myself. And now I was here to usher her out.

When I finally got my car and made my way to the freeway,

the traffic was moving like molasses. In that way sad memories have of linking up, I found myself remembering my father's death. He had been placed in a nursing home after the hospital gave up on him. During a visit there, the social worker recognized me and asked if I would come tell stories. I agreed, but it was a disaster of a performance, with incoherent residents muttering to themselves in wheelchairs pointing in all directions. As I began my first story, a woman toward the back began screaming for the nurse. The cry spread, and before the story was through I had lost half my audience. Yet there was my father, in the front row, hunched over in his wheelchair, craning his neck to see, and loving every minute of it. That was the last time I had seen him alive, and the closest I had come to saying good-bye.

With traffic at a standstill, my mind raced in circles, back to the last time I had seen my mother healthy—at the benefit show I'd done at the temple for her seventieth birthday, when that picture had been taken. I could see her face, lit up with joy, Elijah and Michaela seated on either side of her. That's what I wanted to see, her laughing and smiling. I thought of a joke I'd just received the day before in an e-mail. It was about a Jewish man in England who had been chosen by the queen for knighthood. When she tapped him on the shoulder with her sword, dubbing him Sir Cohen, he was supposed to say certain ancient phrases in Latin. But when the time came, he forgot the Latin words. He panicked for a moment, then said the only words that came to mind, the first of the Four Questions: *"Ma nish-ta-na ha-leila ha-ze?"* The queen looked at him for a moment, puzzled, then asked, "Why is this knight different from all other knights?"

I could almost hear her laughing. It was the sort of joke she would love. The timing was right too; Passover was her favorite holiday, just two weeks away. I wondered if she would live that long.

Lost in thought, I missed my exit. I was frustrated, but relieved as well. With nothing but jokes I couldn't tell, I felt unprepared. I felt like I should at least be wearing my hat; then I remembered that it was gone. I thought of Lenny—what would he have said? I could imagine him smiling and saying, "Here's another gift for you Joel, you lucky guy."

Thinking of gifts reminded me that I'd brought nothing, not even flowers. As I pulled off at the next exit and began winding my way back to the hospital, I spotted a huge shopping center. I managed to find a parking place in the lot and went in to find that they had everything except flowers—at least, not real ones. Plastic roses. Plastic daisies. Plastic chrysanthemums—these, I decided, were worse than nothing. Then, as I was leaving, I spotted something that might be useful—a magic-erase board, the kind you write on, then lift the sheet so the words disappear. It was pink and purple, and on the top was a picture of the Little

Mermaid. It would be just the thing for writing out words she could not hear, as I always did in conversations with my mom.

I couldn't remember where I'd parked my car, so it took some time before I found it and started to drive, only to discover that the hospital was directly across from the shopping center. I drove across the street and parked, looking up at the hospital, finding the fourth floor, trying to guess which was room 413. I dreaded entering the building and the hospital smell I knew would greet me. As I made my way up the elevator, I found myself thinking of a dozen places I'd rather be and a dozen things I'd rather be doing.

I found the door and peeked through the little glass window. And there she was. Half-asleep, tubes in her arms, hair unkempt—she looked terrible. She was dressed in a yellow gown instead of the usual hospital blue or green. The color was most likely intended to brighten things up, but I felt no brightness at all, just a dark inevitability.

I entered quietly and stood at her side, staring at her, for several minutes. "This is my mother," I kept thinking, as though to remind myself. "I'll never see her healthy again." I kissed her softly on the forehead.

Her eyes opened. She spotted me, and I could see her face brighten. "Hello good-lookin', what's cookin'?" she said weakly. It was the way she often greeted me. When I didn't answer she added, "How are you?"

Her face wore a look I knew well, one of hope and expectation. I had seen the look for as far back as I could remember. Tell me something good, it said, brighten up my day. Instead of trying to answer, I shrugged, with a tilt of the head and the "not-so-good" sign. I pointed back to her, as if to say, "And you?"

"Me?" she said, smiling. "I'm doing fine." Even my mom couldn't say this convincingly. "Well, not exactly fine."

I waited.

"Actually, I'm not doing so well. I have late-stage metastatic lung cancer." She hyper-enunciated her words, as though sounding them out to see how she liked them. She didn't, so went on to something cheerier. "Yesterday morning, before surgery, they took me to see the oncologist. Such a nice young woman. Very patient. And she enunciates her words so clearly. Her office is decorated so beautifully, such nice artwork, in all the colors I love. Fall colors."

This, then, was my mother—perhaps the only woman in the world who could see her oncologist and come back excited about how nice the office was. I waited for her to go on. She sighed.

"There are things they could try, like chemo, radiation, but they really won't work. It's gone too far, and too fast." This fit with what I had once been told by a doctor—that, ironically, lung cancer that strikes nonsmokers is the most vicious kind, and when it strikes them, it rips through like a tornado. She waited for me to respond.

Never, in the months since I'd lost it, had I wanted my voice so badly. I could feel the words inside me, trying to push their way out: "Don't worry," I would say. "It will be all right." I would tell her a story, the Passover joke, anything to make her laugh. But I couldn't. Instead I held her hand.

"Joel," she said, "I'm dying."

She looked at me a long time, still waiting for me to speak. I nodded, holding back tears.

"You know," she said, "I'm not afraid of dying. I'm really not. I think it will be like the opening scene in *The Sound of Music*. Do you remember? With Julie Andrews climbing over the hill?"

I nodded again, and she went on. "I think it will be wonderful over there, on the other side. I'll see your father again, but he'll be able to stand up, tall and healthy. And I'll see Grandma Yetta and your Grandpa Izzy, Aunt Dinah and Uncle Sam—everyone will be there, and they'll all be healthy, waiting for me to join them. And they'll call out to me and say—'Welcome, Glady!'—and I'll be able to hear them."

I squeezed her hand and could feel hers squeezing mine back. Then a dark look came over her face, and I could see tears.

"But I don't know how to get there," she said. "The hill is too steep and my suitcase is too heavy to carry . . ." Her voice trailed off, as though in a question, one that she couldn't ask, and I couldn't answer. She was asking me how to die.

We stayed there, silent, for a long time. I thought about that suitcase and what might be inside it. I'd always carried things for my mother—luggage, furniture, groceries. But this was different. I could not carry it for her, nor could she carry it. All she could do was unpack it. And there was only one way to do it— by speaking the truth.

That's when it hit me. I suddenly saw a bicycle, and a basket filled with sand. I could hear Lenny's words. "God is sending you a message . . . something so obvious you can't even see it. . . . It comes down to a single word." *Listen.*

I reached into the plastic bag at my side and pulled out the magic-erase board. Taking the purple stick from its holder, I wrote: "Tell me your story."

The Strawberry

A Zen master had traveled to a distant village. As he was running late for his return train, he decided to take what he thought was a shortcut.

He found himself walking along a steep path at sunset, staring off into the distance. So taken was he by the beauty of the view that he did not notice where he was walking. At that instant he kicked a small stone and, a moment later, realized that he did not hear it land.

He stopped, only to discover that he stood atop a huge cliff. Another step and he would have walked right off, to a hundred-foot drop below.

As he stood there, gazing out at the mountains in the distance, he was suddenly shaken by a loud roar. He turned around to see a huge tiger slowly approaching. He took a step to the side, only to have the ground crumble beneath his feet. Falling off the edge of the cliff, heels over head, his hands reached out to grab whatever might save him. An instant later, he found himself clinging with one hand to a thorny vine, growing out of a crack in the rock. He looked up to the top of the cliff, where he saw the tiger, licking his lips.

His eyes searched far below him, to the bottom of the cliff. There, looking up at him, waited a second tiger.

With one tiger above and another below, he looked again at the vine, its sharp thorns cutting into his hand. Near the vine he saw a tiny hole. Turning his gaze to the hole, he saw a small black-and-white mouse crawl out. It scampered along a tiny ledge to the vine, looked at him for a moment, then looked at the tiger, and finally began to gnaw at the vine.

The monk searched for anything else he might grab, but there was nothing. Then, far off to his side, he spotted a tiny plant. Surely it was too small to hold his weight, but he reached for it just the same. It had green leaves, and as he parted them, he glimpsed something small and red. It was a wild strawberry plant, with one perfectly ripe strawberry.

He plucked it from the plant and ate it. And as he did so he thought, "Isn't life sweet?"

CHAPTER TEN

The Strawberry

My mother read the words on the magic-erase board.

"My story?" she sounded incredulous. "You want to hear *my* story?"

I nodded.

"But I'm not the storyteller." I shook my head. "I wouldn't know where to begin . . ."

"Wherever you start," I wrote, "that's the beginning."

She read my words and nodded. "Anywhere at all?"

I nodded again. She gazed off in the distance for a time, her eyelids slowly closing. When she looked back at me, she was smiling. "I was just thinking about your Grandpa Izzy," she said, "and how much he loved catsup."

I nodded.

"He would put it on everything—eggs, brisket, toast—he said it was his favorite American food." She stopped to laugh, and when she laughed, she coughed, and coughed more, then went on. I heard about his catsup collection, in the basement of the house on Hyde Park, and how he once opened a bottle that had fermented, the catsup shooting straight up to the ceiling. "Forever after, there was a stain on the ceiling. When people would come to the house, we would show it to them . . ."

As she spoke, the room around us faded away—the ugly curtains, the medical instruments, the rolling table, the tray—all of it gone. And what took its place was Cleveland in the days before the Second World War. I heard about the first time she took the streetcar downtown for a chocolate phosphate and what a magical place her cousin Leonard's junkyard was, about her father's mattress factory and the Sunday afternoon trips she would take with him to deliver mattresses in the country.

"Did I ever tell you about the house on Hyde Park?" I shook my head. Of course she'd told me about it, many times, always in passing, as though I must have already known about it. Now I heard about every room and the hallways, the smells of the almond cookies her mother baked, the sycamore trees in the front yard, and the basement. "That's where the cousins club met," she said. "It was me, Norma, Nortie, Morrie, Leonard, Cousin Manny—right under the catsup stain."

I heard about my Uncle Sam, a tiny, gentle, soft-spoken man

who had been married to my Aunt Dinah for seventy-five years. "We were all surprised once, at a party, when he bragged that he was strong enough to tear a phone book in half. He was so small — and it was so unlike him to boast. Everything stopped as the host brought him the Cleveland Yellow Pages and said 'Go ahead!' And he did it — one page at a time!"

They were simple stories, these tales she'd never told me. Even now, she seemed surprised that I wanted to hear them. "I didn't think you'd be interested."

But I was. As she spoke, I was transported — back to a world of delicatessens, and to Uncle Louie, who loved pickles and would take them home in his pocket; back to the pressroom of the *Cleveland Plain Dealer* and her first day as a reporter; and back to summers at Camp Wise, by the lake, where she had been a counselor.

"And one year there was a new counselor, the most handsome young man I'd ever seen. He was tall and dashing, always telling jokes and stories. All the kids loved him. He gave a concert one night, playing his violin — it was beautiful. He said he was going to travel to Palestine to live on a kibbutz . . ."

I had never heard my father described this way. Nor had I ever heard the story of how they'd met, bundled their dreams together, and traveled to California — and what a wonderful place it was. Her stories were peppered with names of the people they'd met, names like Langholz and Schleimer, people I had known all my life. Yet now, in her telling of the years before my brothers and I were born, they became almost mythic. Southern California itself took on a beauty I had never known; I could smell the orange blossoms.

And then it stopped. She simply sighed, coughed some more, and shrugged.

"What else can I say?" she asked.

I thought of Taly's words of advice, about not leaving things unsaid. I thought of the look on Lenny's face when he said, "I think you're stuck in Chelm." I took out the Little Mermaid, pulled off the magic pencil, and wrote "What's in the suitcase?"

She looked at my question, then down by the side of her bed, as though the suitcase were right there, on the floor. She looked back up at me, silently. I could see her eyes pleading *Don't go there.*

But there was nowhere else to go. We had looked under the streetlight and not found it. I waited, and when she still didn't respond, I pulled up the plastic, erasing the words, and wrote "The Truth."

"But it is true—" she protested.

There was no turning back. This time, on the magic-erase board, I wrote "Grandma A."

A look of shock came over her, as though I'd written a dirty word on the board. "But why bring that up now? Why relive that?"

Why indeed? I wondered. And then, once again, I wrote "Suitcase?"

She understood. "Well, she had problems of her own . . ." my mother managed. That had been the line for years.

I nodded for her to go on, though I could see she did not want to. I waited.

"Your father made sure I didn't meet her until the wedding. If I had, I don't think I would have married him. I begged him to stand up to her. He tried, but he couldn't."

My mother shook her head, and I could see the anger surface, only to be forced back down. "She made the best blintzes. Remember?"

I did, and I nodded.

"She gave them to your father, told him not to eat my cooking, said that I was trying to poison him." The anger was back. "She was horrible. She made our lives miserable. She haunted us. She broke into our house. She tortured us. That bitch . . ."

She stopped herself, a look of shock on her face. But it had been done. It was as though she had said a magic word. My mother, who had spent a lifetime never saying anything bad about anyone, had broken the spell. She waited a moment, the sound of "bitch" echoing in the room. She looked a little surprised that lightning didn't strike her. She went on. "She *was* a bitch. She hated me. I don't know why. It wasn't just that I wasn't good enough for her son—she thought that I was the cause of the world's problems. She said I was a Hitler. She spit in my face . . ."

The floodgates had opened. I heard all about my evil grandmother and how she had chased my mother and father to California. About what it was like to live with my father, to watch his dreams crumble as one business after another failed, our family's finances went to pieces, his body fell apart, and the manic depression began to show. He would hatch schemes that she knew would fail, pipe dreams, that would pull us down deeper into debt—"It was like watching the house burn down, slowly, over many years. And I couldn't stop him . . ."

She told me about things that had happened before I was born, things I'd never known. She had been pregnant five times. The other two babies had been girls. One was stillborn and the other, who had been named Mary, died after only one hour. I thought of Michaela, and how my mother's eyes had lit up when she had first held her.

Grief knows no bounds, and hers stretched back through time. Now, she told again of those same idyllic times of her youth, of the house on Hyde Park, but this time I heard of the uncle who had killed himself, the bitter fights, her father's depression and the look on his face when he came back from the electric shock treatments.

I could tell she was exhausted. Her breath was labored and she was coughing. Yet she was exhilarated as well. She had a glow to her, a lightness, that I hadn't seen since I was a kid. I thought it was time to finish and let her rest, but she couldn't stop. She told me how horrible it had been to watch her own father—my Grandpa Izzy—die of lung cancer. "I had flown back to Cleveland. Nat King Cole was there at the same time, in the same hospital. He was also dying of lung cancer. I remember they set up a microphone in Nat King Cole's room, so he could sing to everyone in the hospital. He sang 'Mona Lisa.'"

She turned away, as though looking back through time, and I could see her listening to Nat King Cole's voice. "We all stopped—me, your Grandpa Izzy, your Grandma Yetta, the nurses—it was completely silent. And we all looked up at a speaker. His voice was so smooth, so soft. Even over the hospital's crackly PA system, it sounded like silk."

And there she stopped, with the sound of his voice. She had opened another door, and I knew it would be hard to go through. My mother had spent the past twenty-five years making the best of her hearing loss. Of all those things she had spent a lifetime not complaining about, this was the most painful. I had imagined what it must have been like for her over the years as the volume slipped away. And in all that time, she had not uttered a single word of self-pity. She neither cursed God nor her fate.

I took a deep breath and braced myself for this part of the story. Yet when I looked up to her, she was smiling. I had no idea why.

"I was thinking of Blanche," she explained, "and a concert she took me to last year for my birthday. Actually, I took her—well, I drove." One of my mother's closest friends, Blanche is almost completely blind. "It was at Ambassador Auditorium—they played Beethoven's Sixth Symphony. Pastoral." Her eyes had a dreamy look.

This puzzled me. "Could you hear?" I wrote.

She shook her head. "A little. It all sounded far away. But there are other ways to listen to a concert. I could see it in the way the conductor moved his baton, and the way the instruments followed. I watched Blanche, and I could feel the music coming through her. And then I closed my eyes and I felt it in the arms of my seat. The music was so rich—like whipped cream."

After a time she said, "Isn't it funny, what God takes away from us? And what we get in exchange? When I was young and had my hearing, I always liked music. Hearing your father play the violin, records, dancing. But I've never enjoyed music like I did at that concert."

I was so wrapped up in her description that I didn't notice a nurse had come into the room. She started fiddling with the bags on the IV.

"Oh, how nice," said the nurse, a large woman with big, blonde hair. "You have a visitor."

"My son," explained my mother. "The youngest. He's from Berkeley—he's a professional storyteller."

"A storyteller," she repeated. "Isn't that nice?"

I nodded in agreement.

"And he has a beautiful wife and two beautiful children," my mom added, turning to the side and pretending to spit: *ptew, ptew, ptew*. It was at once comical and endearing to see her spitting to keep away the evil eye, even as she lay dying of cancer. Mercifully, the nurse didn't feel like talking, but went about her business, then left the room.

"And you?" she asked. "What about you? I've done all the talking. How are you, Joel? I've never seen you so quiet." I could see her looking at me, examining my face. "Something's wrong with you, isn't it? You're not well."

I nodded. She had told me her truth, and now I would have to tell her mine.

"Why so quiet?" she asked again. "You haven't said a thing since you got here." Again, I took out the erase board and wrote, "I lost my voice."

A puzzled look appeared on her face. "You have laryngitis?" she asked.

I shook my head. "Cancer," I wrote.

As she read the word, then read it again, her look of puzzlement gave way to a look of horror. "Cancer?" she read. "I don't understand. When? How?"

Then came the questions. A dozen of them. I did my best to answer, writing, erasing, then writing again, until finally she motioned for me to stop and pointed to a small black box at the side of the bed. I brought it over and opened it up. Inside was the tiny microphone with the long wire, the same one we had used in times past, with so little success, when we tried to have conversations in restaurants.

I shook my head. How was this to work?

She plugged one end into another box, which ran up to her hearing aid. "If you whisper very quietly, and enunciate your words, maybe I can hear something."

I tried it. Her face remained expectant, registering nothing, as I whispered, "testing, one, two, three . . ." Then her eyes lit up, as though she had a sudden idea, and she reached over and turned it on. Her hearing aid made a loud squealing sound, and she fiddled with it until it stopped.

"Now try."

I whispered, hyper-enunciating each word. This time she nodded.

"It sounds like you're on top of a mountain, far away. But if you speak very slowly, I can hear you."

I took a deep breath and began my story. After each phrase, I waited for the look of recognition that said she'd understood the words. When she didn't, I would repeat them, stretching my lips around them. Each time she finally heard them, I could see their effect. They tore at her heart. Her face grew darker and darker as she listened. It was painful to watch, made all the harder to do because each time I stopped for another breath, I could hear a voice in my head cry, *What the hell are you doing? It's not enough that your mother is dying—she has to hear all this?*

But I couldn't stop. We had broken the "good-news rule." My life, in her eyes, was like a picture burning. It was the picture of me she had carried in her mind for so many years. I knew it well since I had painted it, carefully, painstakingly, ever since my childhood. It was made of my grades, my performances, my achievements—"Portrait of a Successful Son." Now it was in flames.

When I finished I did something I had not done, had not let myself do, since that morning I'd woken up with no voice. I cried. And my mother did something she had not done for as long as I could remember—she held me. Sick and dying of cancer, she held me, and cared for me, in a way she had not done since I was a child.

We stayed like that a long time. I didn't want to leave. I had found my mother. We didn't say a word, or try. We didn't need to. We had come to one of those times in life when words are not necessary.

Outside it was getting dark. I could tell that my mom was exhausted. She needed to sleep. I let go of her and kissed her forehead. She nodded, understanding that it was time to let go.

Yet she sat there, with a look on her face I had never seen before. She looked like a new mother.

I went out the door. As it closed, I looked back at her one more time, through the little window. *That's my mother,* I said to myself. *My mother.* I liked the sound of the words. And as I looked at her, I could hear her voice again, from years ago, saying what she had said so many times before—"a door closes, a window opens."

STORY ORIGIN: JEWISH, UKRAINE

Hershel's Last Laugh

The great jester, Hershel of Ostropol, died as he lived, with a joke on his lips.

As the end neared, the people of the village gathered around the bed, where he lay weak and almost too tired to speak.

"Hershel," said the rabbi. "You are dying. Now, will you at last be serious?'"

"Why start now?'" asked Hershel.

"But Hershel!" said the rabbi. "In a few minutes, the Angel of Death will come to you. He will ask your name—and what will you say?"

"I'll tell him it's Moses."

"But he'll know it's not Moses—it's Hershel!"

"So if he knew, why did he ask?"

"But he'll ask what you've done with your life, how you've mended your ways, how you've mended the world. What will you say?"

"I'll tell him," said Hershel, "that I've mended my socks."

Hershel began to fade. "I have but one last request," he said, faintly. "Come closer." They all leaned forward. "I ask simply this—when you place me in my coffin, I beg of you—please do not carry me under my arms."

And with these words, he closed his eyes and died.

Silence filled the room. Such a strange request. Then, all at once, they began to ask—"Why? Hershel—tell us why!"

After a moment, Hershel opened his eyes and spoke to them from the world beyond. "I've always been a little ticklish there."

CHAPTER ELEVEN

Hershel's Last Laugh

I TOLD THAT STORY at my mother's funeral, just as I had told it twelve years before, at my father's. It was at her request; she wanted there to be laughter.

"I want it to be a celebration," she said. The ambulance had taken her back to her condominium to await death. "I've been blessed to live the life I've lived. I want to wear my red-and-orange party dress—remember the one I bought for my seventieth birthday?

"You know, I've been to enough funerals with nothing but tears, and so have all my friends. They can cry, but I want them to sing, too, that song from *The Sound of Music,* as loudly as they can, loud enough so I can hear it. And I want them to laugh, too. Joel, will you tell stories?"

The request caught me off guard. I shrugged.

"Like you did when your father died. The same stories — the one about Hershel, and stories of Chelm. Will you?"

I nodded, though I had no idea how I would do it.

"Don't worry," she said. "You can whisper. They'll hear you."

I SPENT THOSE last afternoons with my mother planning out the funeral and listening to her stories. In the evenings, when she drifted off to sleep, I wandered outside, on the streets around her condominium. They were streets I'd always avoided — strip malls in all directions, fast-food restaurants, square cement buildings on square blocks. Around the corner stood a supermarket that sprawled over five acres, and across the street was a shopping center so vast that people would routinely drive to get from one end to the other. I walked alone; there were no other people on the street, just an unending stream of cars.

Yet my mother loved it all — her condominium, the neighbors, and the little stores hidden in the concrete jungle. As I walked I remembered something that had happened many years before, back when my father was dying. I had given my mother a ride somewhere, east along the 10 freeway, halfway to San Bernardino, to pick something up. I don't remember what it was — a form of some sort, something bureaucratic. All I knew was that I resented being there, in the middle of nowhere. We finally came to the place, an adult school, made entirely of concrete blocks, where they told us that whatever she was waiting for was not yet ready, and we would have to wait almost an hour. We sat in a courtyard so hot that we could see vapor lines rising from the ground. Nearby stood a rickety structure that looked like a huge, poorly made shack, surrounded by chicken wire. We waited, her smiling and me stewing, before she finally said, "Isn't it beautiful?"

"Beautiful? What's beautiful?"

She pointed to the chicken-wire structure.

"What is it?"

"It's a birdhouse. See?" I squinted and saw that she was right. "It was built by a class of learning-disabled adults. They haven't put birds in it, but someday they will. Won't that be beautiful?"

Thinking of that birdhouse, then again of my mother, I began to see two pictures. One was of the most ordinary of women, who had lived the life of quiet disappointment that comes when your dreams slip through your fingers. The other was of a woman with a gift for enjoying the meager portions she had been given, for finding the beauty in life where it seemed like there was none to be seen, even at the end of her life, where she had managed to face her own death with a valor I had never seen.

I found myself switching back and forth between the two pictures in my mind, as if it were up to me to choose between them. Then I thought of Lenny and what he might say, were he there.

"Another riddle," he'd say. "And you've got to love the riddle.

Like the case of the two men having a dispute that they take to the Chelm rabbi. After listening carefully, the rabbi strokes his beard and says to one of the men, 'On one hand, you're right . . .' And to the other he says, '. . . and on the other hand, you're right.'

"'But rabbi,' says a third. 'They can't both be right.' To which the rabbi nods and says, 'You're right, too.'

Of course, Lenny would be right. It was not up to me to pass judgment upon her; she was my mother, and I was lucky to have found her after so many years. What mattered was that she loved me and I loved her. And as I realized this, the two pictures became one.

My mother faded fast. Breathing became increasingly wet and difficult, and she could no longer eat. Taly and the kids flew down to say good-bye to her. It was Passover, and because she could not go to a seder, we made an abridged one for her. We did it without food, just songs and stories. Michaela sang the songs she had learned in preschool, about Moses in the river, about Pharaoh and frogs. Elijah sang the Four Questions. Then he told her the story of Passover. It was a beautiful telling, just as I had told it to him the year before. But when he got to the part about Moses being slow of speech, he stopped and added, "Like my daddy."

As my mother listened, no longer able to speak, I could see

the pride in her eyes, first as she watched Elijah, then as she looked at me. I knew well that sense of having her look at me with pride, as she had in so many performances. Those were the looks I had worked so hard all my life to get, that I had responded to with pride of my own. But the look that passed between us was quite different; it was simply a look of recognition.

That night the Angel of Death came for her. The moment she died I awoke from sleep, knowing she was gone. I felt the way anyone feels when their second parent dies, no matter what age they are, and though I didn't say it, Taly knew. "My little orphan," she said, holding me.

EVERY CULTURE HAS its own way of bidding farewell to its dead. In Nepal they place the body on a mountaintop and let the vultures feast upon it, as a reminder that it is merely a soul-less vessel. Inuit tribes will lay the body in a canoe and send it out to sea.

Judaism has ways to remind the mourners that the person really is dead, thereby jump-starting the grieving process. One way to do this is through humor, as sorrow and joy are an inseparable couple, and a little laughter can tickle out the grief. Maybe that is why my mother wanted me to tell stories.

The prospect, though, terrified me. I had not told stories in public since the bar mitzvah in San Francisco, six months before. I was a different person now; I was no longer a performer.

I watched the chapel fill, the faces all familiar. They had watched me do magic shows when I was young, and I knew my mother had told them about my storytelling, yet I'd not seen most of them in years, since my father's funeral, in this same room.

The rabbi came in, a kindly young man who had known my mother well. He hugged me and my brothers, then turned to me, sensing my fear.

"Are you sure you want to do this?" he asked.

I nodded.

"I know it's what she wanted," he said.

When the time came, I stood before the crowd, scanning the faces. Though I knew what stories to tell, I no longer knew how to tell them.

I looked at the rabbi, who nodded, and at my brothers and my aunt. Then I looked again at the faces in the room, faces I had known all my life but had somehow not seen until now. Each one emanated a warmth, a kindness, a decency I had never appreciated. As I looked at them, it was as if a burden were lifted. I thought of Lenny's words—"Let the story flow through your heart." I leaned up close to the microphone and whispered, "Let me tell . . . about my mother's . . . courage."

THE TRADITION AT a Jewish funeral is for the mourners to bury the coffin. "But," the rabbi explained, "we hold the shovel in a special way." He demonstrated, lifting the first shovelful with the shovel facedown. "This reminds us," he said, "that this is not business as usual. We are doing sacred work."

We gathered around the grave and began shoveling, holding umbrellas for one another as a light rain began to fall. One of my mother's oldest friends brought out a letter that my mother had written some thirty-five years before, when my brothers and I were children. Another friend remembered the first time she had met my parents, with all three of us boys jumping on top of the roof of the car.

It's the beauty of stories; whatever you give, you get back more—if you listen. We stood there, around her grave, the tales flowing from them as the rain fell harder.

From time to time I looked at Elijah, who was fascinated with this new digging technique. He showed Michaela, and then two of my mother's friends took turns burying Grandma Gladys, stopping every few shovelsful to wave at the coffin.

"Good-bye, Grandma Gladys. We love you. Have a good time in heaven."

The Happy Man's Shirt

L ong ago in the north of Italy there lived a king who had everything, including a son whom he loved dearly. Yet, for some reason, this son was not happy.

"What can I do?" asked the king. "If there is something that will make you happy, you have only to say it, and it shall be done."

"I do not know," said the son.

"Is there someone you would marry? Whether the richest princess or the poorest peasant, you may do so!"

"I do not know, father," was all the son would say.

The king consulted philosophers, doctors, professors, and priests, asking what might be done to make his son happy. After much discussion, they announced that there was a simple solution. The king must find a man who is completely and truly happy. "Once you find him," they said, "you have only to exchange his shirt for your son's, and thereafter, your son will be happy."

With some relief, the king sent messengers to find a truly happy man. Although they found many who professed to be happy, on closer questioning each proved to be unhappy in some way.

After months of looking, the king began to despair. But one cold day, while out hunting, he heard someone singing in the fields. So sweet and light was the voice that it seemed the singer must be happy. The king looked and saw a young man, bundled against the cold, sitting under a tree.

"Tell me," asked the king. "Are you happy?"

"As happy as can be," said the young man.

"What if you were to come live in the palace? Would you like that?"

"No, thank you, I'm content to be right here."

"What if I was to offer you riches?"

"That's kind of you," said the man, "but I'm happy with what I have."

These words thrilled the king, for he realized that he had, at last, found a truly happy man.

"I must ask you a favor," pleaded the king.

"Anything at all!" replied the youth.

Trembling, the king said, "Come here! Only you can save my son!"

With shaking fingers, the king unbuttoned the man's jacket—and then he stopped.

For the happy man wore no shirt.

Chapter Twelve

The Happy Man's Shirt

When I saw Lenny, three weeks later, he looked like he'd aged twenty years, but he was sober.

"I've spoken the dreaded words," he said. I waited for him to explain. He turned, as though speaking to an imaginary audience. "I said, 'Hi! I'm Lenny!' And right on cue they said, 'Hi, Lenny.' That was twenty-three days ago. I've been going to meetings three times a week and I haven't touched a drop since."

We sat on the porch. I took out the sandwiches I'd brought, not wanting to rely on Lenny's hospitality. "And you? Where on earth have you been?" he asked.

"I have . . . a story."

"A story?" He squinted at me. "You have a story?"

I nodded.

"Let's hear it," he said, biting into the turkey sandwich. "Because I've been waiting."

So I told him all that had happened since I had last seen him. As he listened he looked away, his eyes glazing over, as if he were there with me, in the hospital, in my mother's condominium, and at the cemetery.

I told him of the stories I told at the funeral, of the suitcase and the birdhouse, of Chelm and Hershel. I also told him about what happened afterward. I had wanted to take Taly and the kids to see the house where I'd grown up. Though I'd heard the place had been bought and sold several times, it was a shock to see it. The house looked terrible, no longer the cream color I remembered, but a sickly shade of green, with chunks of stucco coming loose. Bodies of old cars lined the driveway. The two huge elm trees in the front yard had been cut down, leaving only stumps. The flowers that my mother had planted and my father had loved—birds-of-paradise—had died out, leaving only weeds. I had planned to knock on the door, to explain how I had once lived there, and ask if I might look around. But instead we sat in the car, rain splattering the windshield, and I realized I no longer wanted to see it.

It was a mistake going back, I told myself, as I drove us back to the freeway. Then something caught my eye. There was a man on a bicycle, wearing a red sweater, riding around in circles. I slowed down to see him, and he looked up at me, a happy but puzzled look on his face. A moment later I saw a smile, then a wave, and I waved back.

When I finished my story I could see that Lenny was smiling, too. He began to speak, then stopped himself. Again he started, and again he stopped. For the first time since I'd known him, Lenny had nothing to say.

We waited silently for a long time before I asked the question that had been on my mind. "How can . . . I thank . . . you?"

He shook his head. "It is for me to thank you for letting me in. You have given me exactly what I wanted—a story, and a damn good one at that. Thank you."

GRIEF HAS A WAY of bringing out the sweetness in life, and the days of that late spring were ones that I will always remember. The rains that had drenched Northern California, well beyond winter, ended abruptly. Within a week the cherry trees, which had been struggling to blossom for months, burst into bloom.

With my mother gone, I found myself drawn to things that reminded me of her—the teal-blue Hoover upright vacuum cleaner I had inherited, her electric typewriter, and a forest-green mahjongg set that had belonged to her mother. In the back room of my office I sorted through her letters to me, stacks of them. Some of them, I'm ashamed to say, were still unopened. Knowing that she would never write me again, I opened them slowly. Most contained brief chatty notes, written on her typewriter, which punched holes where the lowercase e's should have been. In addition to the notes, I found numerous clippings—articles that mentioned names of my old high-school teachers, some comic strips, and several of Erma Bombeck's columns. Among the clippings, one stood out. It was an account of a concert by Itzhak Perlman, written by Jack Riemer of the *Houston Chronicle*. She had written a note to me at the top: "Joel—thought you would enjoy this story."

On Nov. 18, 1995, Itzhak Perlman, the violinist, came onstage for a concert at Avery Fisher Hall at Lincoln Center in New York City.

If you have ever been to a Perlman concert, you know that getting onstage is no small achievement for him. He was stricken with polio as a child and so he has braces on both legs and walks with the aid of two crutches.

To see him walk across the stage one step at a time, very deliberately, and slowly, is an event. He walks painfully, yet majestically, until he reaches his chair. Then he sits down, slowly, puts his crutches on the floor, undoes the clasps on his legs, tucks one foot back and extends the other foot forward. Then he bends down and picks up the violin, puts it under his chin, nods to the conductor and proceeds to play.

By now, the audience is used to the ritual. They sit quietly while he makes his way across the stage to his chair, they remain reverently silent while he undoes his clasps on his legs. They wait until he is ready to play.

But this time, something went wrong. Just as he finished the first few bars, one of the strings on his violin broke. You could hear it snap — it went off like gunfire across the room.

There was no mistaking what that sound meant. There was no mistaking what he had to do. People who were there that night thought to themselves: "We figured that he would have to get up, put on the clasps again, pick up the crutches and amble his way offstage — to either find another violin or else find another string for this one."

But he didn't. Instead, he waited a moment, closed his eyes and then signaled the conductor to begin again. The orchestra began, and he played from where he had left off. And he played with such passion and such power and such purity as they had never heard before. Of course anyone knows that it is impossible to play a symphonic work with just three strings. I know that, and you know that, but that night Itzhak Perlman refused to know that. You could see him modulating, changing, recomposing the piece in his head. At one point, it sounded like he was de-tuning the strings to get new sounds from them that they had never made before.

When he finished, there was an awesome silence in the room. And then people rose and cheered. There was an extraordinary outburst of applause from every corner of the auditorium. We were all on our feet, screaming and cheering, doing everything we could to show how much we appreciated what he had done.

He smiled, wiped the sweat from his brow, raised his bow to quiet us, and then he said, not boastfully, but in a quiet, pensive, reverent tone, "You know, sometimes it is the artist's task to find out how much music you can still make with what you have left. . . ."

THE SCHOOL YEAR ENDED as it had begun, with tears. This time they did not come from Michaela, but from Taly and me. On a bright Wednesday in June, Elijah received his kindergarten diploma. The next day Michaela finished her first year of preschool. Proudly she marched with her class across the schoolyard, into the next year's classroom.

I, too, had a graduation; the following week I went in for my follow-up cancer scan. I lay there, completely still, listening to the machine beep as I moved forward, a millimeter at a time.

Then the nurse unstrapped me and I went down the hall to the radiologist for the results. I found him sitting behind a desk covered with X-rays and charts, a soft-spoken Chinese man with big wire-rimmed glasses.

"Mr. ben Izzy?" he said. I nodded, waiting. "Well, I have good news. The test came out negative. You're squeaky clean." Hard as it had looked, the radiologist explained, the machine had found nothing at all — there was no trace of cancer. Nor was there any reason to believe it would return.

I couldn't respond, but merely stood there, staring at him. He seemed to think I didn't understand, so he cleared his throat and said, "The cancer's gone."

I nodded, but still could not react. I realized that the news meant nothing until I could share it with Taly. I rushed home where I found her waiting, anxiously. When she saw my face I didn't have to say a thing. She broke into tears and we held each other for a long time, and I wondered how it could possibly be that we felt close to one another. It was all strangely paradoxical; our lives had turned upside down, the glass was still broken, but there we were.

We felt especially close two weeks later when we reached the next milestone — Elijah's sixth birthday, a year to the day since I had learned of my cancer. There was reason to celebrate, to be sure, but also a sadness, as I felt my mother's absence. She had always sent birthday gifts for the kids, usually books that followed their interests, along with cards that had pictures of rabbits, clowns, and balloons. I thought of her every day now, forcing myself to believe that she was actually gone. Over time I have managed to convince myself of this, though to this day I still have trouble accepting the fact that she never calls.

As we ate Elijah's birthday dinner, I looked at my family, thinking of all that had happened in the past year. Elijah's interest in flags had faded away and then returned, and there were, once again, flags all around the table. He had grown several inches, and his head full of curls had turned from blond to brown. He had also become a terrific storyteller. Always a little shy, he told his stories only to Michaela. True, most of his stories were about Beanie Babies, but in time his repertoire would broaden. For now they were just right, and as he told them, she sat listening, looking at him as though he were the sun in the sky.

While she watched him, Taly and I watched them both. Children are miracles—something we realize when they're born, but must struggle to remember each day. And though Taly rarely told them stories, I noticed something I hadn't heard from her before—singing. They were beautiful, soft songs, and I would listen from outside the kids' door on nights when she put them to bed. Some were tunes she made up on the spot, improvising words, while others were favorites from musicals, like *Fiddler on the Roof.* The kids would learn the songs and sing along. One night, long after Elijah should have been asleep, I walked by the door to their room and heard his little voice singing, "If I were a rich man, yidle-diddle-didle . . ."

I listened to him, thinking of our own finances. I had begun to find work here and there as a freelance writer, and though it was a struggle, we were managing. Even so, I felt like a rich man, not in terms of money, but as described in the Talmud, where it asks "Who is rich?" and answers "The one who can appreciate what he has." The line from the Talmud reminded me of the experts' expert and how he had said the silent rabbi in my throat perhaps knew a secret. Maybe that was the secret — and the lesson I'd needed to learn.

Although one can never be sure where one story ends and another story begins, it seemed to me that this story had come to its ending. While it may not have been the simple, happy ending that I had craved, in its own way it was better. I had arrived at something more enduring than happiness, a feeling that only comes with time and loss — and wears no shirt.

TOWARD THE END of summer I received one more gift. This one came in a large cardboard box, bearing the return address of a law firm in San Jose, whose name I did not recognize. The box was very light for its size, and sure enough it was filled mostly with Styrofoam popcorn. At the top was a manila envelope, addressed to me.

"Dear Mr. ben Izzy," the letter inside began. "Pursuant to the will of the late Dr. Leonard Feingold, we are sending you the enclosed . . ." A wave of shock washed over me as I sifted through the popcorn, finding only a delicate pink wineglass. Looking again in the envelope I saw another letter, on yellow legal paper, written by hand.

> There was once a Zen master of great renown. He lived in a monastery, and had rid himself of all worldly possessions except one—a magnificent wineglass, which he treasured. Each day he would marvel at the glass, commenting on its beauty as the light shone through it. He always showed it off to visitors who came to the monastery.
>
> This surprised the other monks, who were angered to see their master so attached to a material object. One day they confronted him.
>
> "Great master," said one. "How can you take pleasure from a thing such as this? Can you not see that it is merely an object—something transitory? A thing that can be easily broken?"
>
> The master looked at the glass and smiled. "Of course. In fact, in my mind the glass is already broken. And so I enjoy it all the more."
>
> Lenny

S T O R Y   O R I G I N :   J E W I S H ,   R O M A N I A

The Fox in the Garden

A hungry fox wandering through the woods came upon a high wall. He walked along it for some time, until he discovered it went in a huge circle.

Curious as to what was inside, he searched for an opening. Finally, he found a small hole. Through it, he spied a most magnificent garden, filled with sweet-smelling flowers, succulent melons, and bunches of ripe red grapes.

He desperately wanted to go inside, but the hole was too small. After trying again and again to squeeze in, he realized it was useless. Yet, so great was his desire to enter that he came upon an idea.

He would fast until he was thin enough to pass through the hole. With that plan, he waited there for three days, starving himself, until he barely managed to slip in.

Once inside, he found the garden to be more wondrous than it had seemed from the outside. He feasted on its fruits and had the time of his life.

All went well for some time, until he heard someone else in the garden. It soon became clear that they were hunting for him.

The fox realized he must escape, but he had grown too fat to fit through the hole. So, once again, he had to fast. This time, it was all the more difficult, for he was surrounded by all the foods he craved. After three very long days, he managed to squeeze out.

Once outside, he stopped to look back through the hole. "Ah, life," he said, "your simple pleasures are too much for me—but worth it, just the same."

Chapter Thirteen

The Fox in the Garden

As we go through life, each new loss recalls those that came before it. Lenny's passing left a hole in me, and I ached from its hollowness. Yet there was a fullness as well, for each time I thought of him, another of his stories would come back to me. Those stories seemed to weave into my own, a tale whose twists, I believed, I finally understood. Once again, I was wrong.

In Liberia they have a saying: You cannot unsneeze a sneeze. Similarly you cannot stop a story from unfolding, once it begins. Storytellers talk about the "rule of three" that runs through stories—three bears, three sons, three wishes, and so on. So I suppose it was destined that I should receive a third phone call, from a third doctor. It came in September, coincidentally enough, on my birthday.

"Hello, Mr. Storyteller? How are you?" It took me a moment to recognize the accent of the experts' expert. He had been thinking about me, he said, and wanted to see me. In truth, though I liked him, I would have been quite happy never to see another doctor as long as I lived. But he was adamant, so I made the appointment and went in.

When I arrived he introduced me to another doctor, who asked if he might examine me. From the moment I met him, this doctor struck me as different from the others I'd met. He was a soft-spoken Latino man, and he reminded me of someone, though I couldn't exactly say whom. He spoke with great patience, as if he had time — a rare quality in doctors, especially surgeons, which is what he turned out to be. He felt my neck and peered down my throat, as so many others had done before. Finally he said, "Perhaps I may be able to help."

His words shocked me, not just for the content, but for the lack of arrogance. He'd said "may." It was then that I realized what he reminded me of — a doctor. Not one I'd ever met, but one I'd only imagined. He told me about a strange procedure called a "thyroplasty," which involved sticking a piece of a plastic — which he described as an oddly shaped Lego — inside my neck, thereby pushing my paralyzed vocal cord back to the center, so the other could vibrate against it. While it would not bring the vocal cord back to life — nothing could do that — it might offer some improvement in the sound.

"The difference," chimed in the expert, rather poetically, "would be like that of an oboe and a clarinet. One has two reeds, the other has one, but both can make beautiful music."

Though I've always loved the sound of the clarinet, and I appreciated the metaphor, I was wary of the surgery. A permanent Lego in my throat did not sound appealing. It was not hard to imagine the possibilities of having my voice return—indeed, I had spent months dreaming of just that. But before moving forward, I desperately wanted to know what would happen if it went wrong.

The surgeon nodded. Of course, he said, the procedure did not come with a guarantee. While it might improve my voice, it could also make it worse. If it failed, I could lose my whisper. I would then be entirely mute. Then there were "possible complications." I remembered reading the list of "possible complications" before my first surgery, which spanned the gamut from slight discomfort to sudden death. I didn't just want to see a list—I wanted to hear from someone on whom this procedure had failed. He gave me the name of another patient—a former high-school basketball coach. Like me, he had lost his voice due to a paralyzed vocal cord, in his case caused by a rare viral infection. He had undergone this same procedure, but the results had been less than satisfactory.

It was only after several weeks of procrastination that I mustered up the nerve to call the number.

"Hello?"

I thought it was the voice of a young girl. "Is your . . . father home?" I asked.

There was a long pause. "He passed away . . . twenty years ago. May I . . . help you?"

I couldn't believe what I had done. I blurted out seven or eight apologies before he stopped me. "That's alright . . . it happens . . . all the time."

I finally managed to explain why I was calling, and he told me his story. I had to push the phone against my ear, as his words were barely audible. The operation had been a failure. ". . . a delicate procedure . . . there were complica . . ."—his voice trailed off, and I could hear him gasping for breath—". . . cations."

"Will you . . . try again?"

There was another long pause. "No, it's . . . a mess . . . down there. Scar tissue. I had . . . one shot . . ." He trailed off. A few seconds later he said, "I've learned . . . to live . . . with it."

I finished the conversation, hung up, and a chill ran through my body. The operation would mean rolling the dice all over again, and the thought was very scary.

THOUGH I WAS FRIGHTENED, Taly was terrified.

"The day you lost your voice, I began hoping against hope that it would return." It was a Sunday afternoon and the kids were with a baby-sitter while we hiked through the Presidio in

San Francisco. The former army base is one of the greenest parts of the city, leading down to the base of the Golden Gate Bridge. "You have to understand how much I wanted your voice to return. I prayed for it, and it didn't come back.

"Finally, after so many months, that hope died. It was a slow, awful death. And then I buried it. I had to. There was nothing else I could do." She was quiet for a time, shaking her head.

"And now, you're asking me to exhume it?" She was crying. We had come to a place under the bridge where a cold wind surrounded us, drying her tears in their tracks. "It's too painful. I already feel like a burnt forest."

There was no point in arguing with her. For all the ways poets and storytellers have sung the praises of hope, the truth is that it stings. Hope, the Greek myth tells us, was brought into the world by Pandora. It lay at the bottom of the box that she was not supposed to open. Of course, she did open it, releasing any number of horrible things into the world. And afterward, all that remained in the box was hope. I had always thought of this story as extolling the virtues of hope—the great consolation prize. Yet now, as I thought of what I'd been through, and listened to Taly, hope seemed like another one of the horrible things Pandora unleashed, perhaps the cruelest among them. We had both been burned by the hope that my voice might return.

"How can we open that door again?" she asked, and waited

for an answer. When one didn't come, she went on. "But I can't close it either. It's your voice. And your decision.

"But I want you to know something. And this isn't easy to say." She took hold of my hands. "Joel, I love you. And I'll love you no matter what. But I like you better now. I like who you've become."

We stood in silence for a long time, as a wind blew in from the bay and indecision whirled around inside my head. I had no idea what to do. I looked at a sailboat passing under the bridge and then into Taly's eyes, which were smiling.

I AGONIZED FOR several days, and it was then that I really began to miss Lenny. I found I had questions I wanted to ask him; for one thing, I had read through the entire book of Job, three times, and could not find where God laughed. I had written the law office after I'd received the package with the glass and was informed that he'd died suddenly at the start of the summer, of a second heart attack. At Lenny's request there had been no funeral, and he'd been buried in the cemetery in Santa Cruz, beside Pearl.

Yet, even with Lenny gone, I could still hear his voice, and imagine what he'd say about my dilemma were he alive. First he would laugh, a long, hard laugh. Finally, when he finished, I could hear him say, "And you came here to tell me, once again, that I was right, right?"

"Right?"

"Right," he would say again, this time nodding, and pointing upward. "I said that your story was in the hands of a masterful storyteller." I would push him for advice, as to whether I should get the operation or not, and he would say, "As I see it, either way you have to lose something—and that's good. As I've said before, you are one lucky man."

THE SURGEON HAD EXPLAINED that I would need to be awake for the procedure, so that he and the expert could "tune" my voice. They would try out various pieces inside my throat to see if one would work. "But do not worry," he assured me as nurses strapped me down to a table and filled me with drugs. "You will feel no pain."

I heard two nurses talking about their plans for Thanksgiving the next day and then the sound of a clarinet, playing a familiar tune. I finally recognized it, and my own voice, which followed, from the tape of stories I had given to the expert. "Alright," he said, "this is how we want him to sound."

It didn't take long for the drugs to take effect; a few minutes later I found myself marveling at how brightly the lights in this operating room glistened off the blade of the scalpel, just so. Someone covered my face with a folded towel, and I felt as if I were in a spa. There was a lot of fiddling around my neck, and then I heard the surgeon's soft voice say, "Alright, let's try it," to which the expert responded, "Mr. Storyteller, please count to five."

I tried to oblige—and nothing came out. Absolutely nothing. Not my whisper, not my croak, nothing at all. Instantly I felt something else surge through my veins, and my drug-induced sense of ease vanished.

"Not that one," said the surgeon. There was sudden action around my neck, during which I could hear my panic approaching, like a far-off train. Finally I heard the expert's voice say, "Alright, let's try again. Count to five."

Again I tried—nothing. But it was worse than before. Not only was there no sound but I couldn't breathe. "He's pulling at the restraints," someone shouted. There was some rapid fiddling and the sound of footsteps, and I was able to breathe again, which I did in short gusts of panic.

I heard whispers and the sound of hushed arguing. Someone said, "I don't think so," and someone else said, "Just one more time." There was more activity around my neck.

"Please, Mr. Storyteller," said the expert. "One more time. Count to five."

Suddenly I heard numbers, loud numbers, echoing through the room. "One, two, three . . ." I stopped, and they stopped—there was just the echo of "three." I started again, and they came out loud and clear, filling the room—I was shouting! The room filled with applause. When I got to ten, I called out "YES!"

"Excellent! And now, please, tell us a story."

Maybe it was the drugs. Or maybe it was the shock of hearing my own voice. But, for the life of me, I could not come up with a thing. He'd asked for a story, any story, and I could not think of a single one. I could hear the silence as everyone waited and then, very softly, I felt a story tap me on the shoulder. A moment later, a picture came into mind, of a desert, and in the distance, a palace. Through the doorway of the palace I could see a crowd of people and, before them, on a throne, sat a king.

"Let me tell you a tale of long ago, from the old city of Jerusalem, back in the days when Solomon was king . . ." The room erupted in applause and cheering. I wanted to go on but I heard something that made me stop. Somewhere, in the midst of the clapping and shouting, I heard a voice, a still, quiet voice, laughing. I strained my eyes to find its source, but could see only the towel.

"Enough!" said the expert. All the noise stopped. Then I heard the surgeon's soft voice say, "Sutures."

I COULD NOT contain my euphoria as they rolled me into the recovery room.

"Hi, there!" I said to the nurse. "Nice day, isn't it! I like the hat! Great hospital you got here." Then, to a patient, "Wow, that's some cast you got there! Hope it heals soon!" I blathered to the right of me and to the left of me, to everyone in the room.

When I was moved to a corner and all alone for a moment, I broke into "Singin' in the Rain," which stopped abruptly when I spotted the expert across the room.

"Hey, doctor!" I shouted. "You looking for me? I'm over here!"

He had a huge grin on his face. "So," he said. "About that story . . ."

"You want to hear it? Let me tell you! It's about King Solomon and how he was tricked into removing his ring by Ashmodai, King of the Demons . . ."

He motioned for me to stop. "It seems," he said, "the procedure is a success. But there is something you must understand. In order for us to place the device in your throat, we needed to give you anti-inflammatory drugs. We gave you just enough to last through the operation. Within a few minutes they will wear off, and swelling will set in, as is to be expected. The swelling will last for approximately three weeks. And then, you will have the voice you have now.

"But—and this is very important—during these three weeks, you must not talk, or even try to talk."

I stared at him.

"You see, the placement of the device is very precise. Listening to your voice now, and comparing it to the voice on your tapes, I believe we have an excellent correction, as good as any I have ever heard. But to keep it that way, it must heal into place exactly as we set it. Any talking during this time—even whispering, as you have been doing until now—could dislodge it. And I am afraid that could permanently damage your voice."

It took a moment for his words to register. "You mean that now that I can talk, I can't talk?"

He nodded.

"But there's so much I want to say! To tell everything . . ."

He stopped me again, with a motion of his hand. "I have a gift for you." He reached into his shirt pocket and pulled out a pen, which he handed to me. "This is for you. So now you can tell the whole story, about King Solomon and everything else."

STORY ORIGIN: SUFI MUSLIM, TURKEY

The Secret of Happiness

Nasrudin is known as much for his wisdom as his foolishness, and many are those who have sought out his teaching.

One devotee tracked him down for many years before finding him in the marketplace sitting atop a pile of banana peels—no one knows why.

"Oh great sage, Nasrudin," said the eager student. "I must ask you a very important question, the answer to which we all seek: What is the secret to attaining happiness?"

Nasrudin thought for a time, then responded. "The secret of happiness is good judgment."

"Ah," said the student. "But how do we attain good judgment?"

"From experience," answered Nasrudin.

"Yes," said the student. "But how do we attain experience?"

"Bad judgment."

Chapter Fourteen

The Secret of Happiness

THAT WAS FIVE YEARS AGO. When I look back at those three weeks, they seem like the moment just after waking from a dream, when you can close your eyes and slip back into it.

Even as I counted the minutes until I would again be able to speak, I knew that I would be losing something. Just as I had lost my voice some five hundred days before, I would now be losing a certain quiet, a loss that had given me so much. So I spent much of my anxious, self-enforced silence trying to remind myself of those lessons I'd learned, writing down those things I wanted to remember when I awoke.

Three weeks to the day after surgery was the first night of Hanukkah. We gathered around the menorah Elijah and I had made out of small brass elbow-joints. Taly held Michaela's hand as she lit the first candle. We sang the blessings, then Elijah asked for a story.

"A story?" I said. "Alright, I'll tell you the story of Hanukkah."

My voice felt and sounded exactly as it had in the hospital during the second surgery, just as it had before the first.

I told them the story of a miracle, of a light that, by all rights, should have burned out—but did not. Instead, it burned for eight days and nights, and it was burning at that moment on the windowsill, reflected in their faces. They stood there for a time, looking at the glass, before Michaela asked for another story. I thought for a time before it came to me.

"Have I ever told you about your Great-Grandpa Izzy—and how he used to love catsup?"

So began the stories I told them, and tell them, to this day. My voice is fine now, strong and healthy. There has been no sign of the cancer. I'm back at work, telling stories. And when I look back at those days when my voice was missing, they seem like time spent in another world.

In that world, my mother is alive and well. Lenny is talking in riddles and playing his tricks. Elijah is, once again, that five-year-old boy with curly blond hair and Michaela is a baby. Taly and I sit on the back porch of our house, watching the leaves fall, basking in an innocence that we don't even realize we have.

Once you open doors backward through time, other doors appear. Behind one stands my father, tall and handsome, in his white dinner jacket, playing the violin. And my mother is that young, bright-eyed girl in Cleveland, sitting at the feet of my Grandpa Izzy, listening to a story.

And so I drift back and forth between this world and that, looking for answers to the same questions I have asked all along: Why did this happen? Was it all meant to be, part of some great plan?

That's what Lenny thought. I can still hear his voice: "Is there a reason? Of course! Everything has a reason. You, me, we're all part of a magnificent story, in which each of us plays a part. It's a tapestry with so many threads winding in and out that only God-on-high could ever weave it."

I'd like to believe he's right. That would explain why God laughs; there *is* a reason, and if only we knew the reason, we'd laugh, too.

Taly thinks the idea is ridiculous. "No way. Even if God does exist, she's not up there micromanaging the details of your life."

She's right, of course. To imagine God up there, pulling strings on a bazillion stories here on earth—it's far too complicated. And way too simple. No, I just can't believe it.

But I can't go the other way, either, saying that things happen for no reason at all. To do so would mean leaping into a void filled with randomness and meaninglessness.

Here is what I've come to: I still believe that things in this world do, indeed, happen for a reason. But sometimes that reason comes only *after* they happen. It is not a reason we find, but one we carve, sculpted from our own pain and loss, bound together with love and compassion. As hard as we may search, we can only see it when we stop to wonder, looking back to see where we've been and what we've learned. It's a grueling process, this forging a reason from the stuff of life, but it's all we can do. And what we get for our efforts is a story.

WHAT, THEN, OF the secret of happiness? I know stories that touch upon it and even one by that name. But for me, the secret of happiness sits atop a long list of life's secrets. Perhaps that's the secret—there is no secret of happiness. Yet, we keep searching, maybe because the simple act of looking for it makes us happy.

As for the beggar king—that's another story.

The Beggar King

IT WAS AFTER A LIFETIME of wandering that Solomon found himself alone, in a boat — an old man adrift at sea. He spent his days fishing, and marveling on all that had happened since that distant day, so many years before, when Ashmodai had cast him halfway across the world, to the midst of a vast desert.

He had been forced to make his way as a beggar, wandering from place to place, trying to find someone who would believe that he was really a king. Finally he gave up and simply tried to convince them he was hungry. He lived off the scraps of food he could beg, and he eventually found work, as a cook for another king. But he lost that job in shame and was banished to die in the wilderness. He would have, too, had he not been captured as a prisoner by a band of thieves, who sold him as a slave to a blacksmith. It was after seven long years that he earned his freedom, along with a single bag of gold. This, he used to buy a boat, hoping it would carry him back to his beloved Jerusalem.

He had set sail with fair winds, but those had died just one month into his journey. Nor had they returned, and with no land in sight, it slowly began to dawn upon him that it was here, at sea, lost and forgotten, that his life would end.

The realization surprised him, as had every twist and turn his journey had taken. Yet nothing surprised him quite so much as what he had come to feel—a simple sense of peace. At last, he had come to accept what life had handed him.

It happened one day, as he sat lost in thought, that he felt a tug on his line. It came from a huge fish, so large, in fact, that it dragged the boat back and forth, this way and that, for many hours, before Solomon pulled in a huge shark—the largest he had ever seen. As he cleaned it out, he saw that its belly contained other fish it had eaten, including one of a sort he had never seen before, a small blue fish. Though old and on the verge of death, he was still curious to learn. He cut this fish open, too —and stopped. For inside he saw something shiny, something golden—a ring. His ring.

He held it up to the light, recognizing the writing on the inside, the secret name of God. Then, ever so slowly, he slid the ring onto his finger.

Instantly, he found himself dressed in fine robes, seated in a comfortable chair, inside a magnificent palace. All around he saw guards, standing at attention, with Beniah, his chief guard, to his right. And to his left stood a tall blue demon—Ashmodai—locked in chains, who spoke.

"Well, your highness. We're waiting! Are you going to answer the question?"

Solomon was too stunned to speak. Finally, he said, "Question? What question?"

"Why, the question I asked you nearly one hour ago!"

"One hour? Why, it's been nearly fifty years . . ."

Beniah spoke up. "Your highness, I'm afraid you have been sitting there, in silence, for one hour. You may wish to answer the question . . ."

"The question. Yes, Ashmodai, would you repeat the question?"

"Certainly, your highness. Have you learned something about illusion?"

Solomon said nothing for a long time. Then, slowly, he nodded to Ashmodai. "Yes, I have. You may go."

With that, the Demon King laughed one last laugh and began to shrink, smaller and smaller, until he was no larger than a chicken. He slipped from his chains, flew three times around the palace, out of a window, and over the temple that Solomon had built, never to be seen again.

Solomon went back to ruling his kingdom, but was a different man. Gone was his arrogance, evaporated were his illusions of grandeur. From that day on, he showed a wisdom he had not known before—a wisdom of the heart. He knew how it felt to be loved by all and how it felt to be lost and alone, without a friend in the world. He knew what it was to have everything— and what it was to have nothing. For he had been both a beggar —and a king.

About the Stories

TRACING THE LINEAGE of folktales is a tricky business. They travel so much that, in the end, we're usually left wondering just where, when, and how any given story first came to be told. In the following pages I tell a little about the stories that appear before each chapter of the book. I have tried to say something about their origin, when known, as well as how I first came to learn them.

The Beggar King (pages 1–10 and 213–16)

Originally from the Babylonian Talmud, tractate Gittin, this tale has appeared in many variations over the years. The legend of the magical stonecutting powers of the worm known as the Shamir seems to have grown out of the biblical restriction against using metal to build the holy arc of the covenant.

This tale echoes others known in Muslim countries, and the same Ashmodai may be from the Persian Asehma-Daeva, the demon Aeshma. In *Jewish Folktales* selected and retold by Pinhas Sadeh, (Anchor Books, 1989), the author speculates that the tale of Solomon's wanderings may be a metaphoric recounting of King David's wanderings among the Philistines, during which time he pretended to be insane.

In the abbreviated version of the story that appears in this book, I have drawn upon several different texts and included some touches of my own. I first learned of the story from Howard Schwartz's groundbreaking work of Jewish folklore, *Elijah's Violin and Other Jewish Fairy Tales* (Harper and Row, 1983), which I recommend along with Sadeh's book to anyone who would like to read a fuller version of this story and other stories about Solomon and Ashmodai, king of the demons.

The Lost Horse (page 11)

Generally attributed to Lao Tzu, author of the *Tao Te Ching*, this tale expresses one of the core tenants of Taoism. The story seems to have been further shaped by the poet and prince Liu An, (179–122 B.C.E.) in his book *Huai Nan Tzu*.

I heard frequent references to this story during my travels in Hong Kong and China; when something went wrong people would say *sai weng shih ma*—the old man lost his horse.

I first heard the story from a psychic in the Mission District of San Francisco, and was later given a written version by story-teller Ruth Stotter.

The Cricket Who Jumped to the Moon (page 29)

This original tale was inspired by memories of my father. I also drew upon a motif I found in a Burmese folktale, "The Musician of Tagaung," which told of a boy whose father dreamed he would someday become the greatest harp player Burma had ever known. The boy tried and tried to play the harp, but had no talent for it, breaking the strings and ruining harp after harp. It was many years later, long after his death, that people found the broken harps, and began to invent stories of his musical abilities. So it was, over time, that he became known as a great harp player.

Optimism and Pessimism (page 49)

Though this story is quite well known, tracking down its origins was quite a challenge. I finally found what seems to be its earliest known written ancestor in a strange little book, buried deep within the stacks of the San Francisco Main Library. The book seems to be a story in itself; its title page was so intriguing that it seems worth reprinting here:

Waggish Tales of the Czechs
Originally entitled
Gesta Czechorum

Done into English out of the original 15th Century Czech manuscript of Rehor Frantisek, of Czaslau, sometime Almoner to the count of Zikmund, King over both Bohemia and Hungary, and Holy Roman Emperor, and later Master of the Wardrobe to the Magnata Bohdan Beverlik of Tynist by C. D. S. Feals, in an adaptation to the reading requirements of the American public by

Norman Lockridge

The Candide Press

1947

Therein lies a tale entitled "A Peasant Boy's Faith," in which three rich children attempt to play a dirty trick on a poor, but earnest, boy by leaving horse manure in his Christmas stocking. He responds by saying that he was given a horse by Santa.

I've known this story for many years, but cannot remember when I first heard it.

The Vow of Silence (page 61)

This appears to be a variant of a tale popular in Finland—also recorded in Norway and Ireland—known as "Too Much Talk," about three men who retreat to a quiet glen at the far end of the world, taking a vow of silence. After seven years the first one speaks: "I heard a cow lowing." The other two are angry but silent. Then, seven years later, the second says, "It was not a cow, but a bull!" Seven years after that the third says, "I'm leaving this place. There's too much talk!"

I first heard the story, while I was a student at Stanford, from Nick Burbules, the resident associate in my co-op.

The Search for Truth (page 81)
Since hearing this story from Lenny, I have tried to track down its origins without success. Though I have found written versions of it, the authors of those have also been unable to track down the source, which seems to be as elusive as truth itself. I attribute it to India merely because the story mentions the country; I would welcome information from anyone who knows more.

The Border Guard (page 97)
Like many of the shorter stories in this book, versions of this tale are often attributed to Sufi trickster Mullah Nasrudin. Sometimes, instead of a bicycle, he has a wheelbarrow full of sand.

I had heard this story long before Lenny told it to me, from my friend Charlie Lenz, an Austrian who lives in Switzerland near the Austrian border, where he teaches karáte.

The Appointment (page 107)
Known in many variations throughout Middle Eastern folklore, this tale became the namesake for John O'Hara's 1934 novel,

Appointment in Samarra. O'Hara heard the stories from William Somerset Maugham who also wrote a well-known literary version of the tale, with the story told from Death's perspective.

I knew the story before Lenny told it to me, having first heard it in 1989 from Dr. August Zemo, headmaster of the Riverside School in Thalwil, Switzerland, where I served briefly as a storyteller-in-residence.

The Wisdom of Chelm (page 127)

These are but a few of the many tales about the mythical Jewish town of fools. There is, in fact, an actual city of Chelm in modern-day Poland, forty miles to the east of Lublin. Though the city once had a sizable Jewish population, no one knows just how it came to be associated with foolishness.

Many of the tales told of Chelm are told of other villages of fools as well, including Gotham in England, Mols in Denmark, Schildburg in Germany, and Kampen in Holland. After hearing my mother refer to the Chelm stories, I was formally introduced to them by Mrs. Bertha Molatsky, my second-grade religious-school teacher and the librarian at the Temple City Library. Seeing I was bored stiff, she sent me to read *Zlateh the Goat and Other Stories* by Isaac Bashevis Singer, for which I am forever grateful.

Buried Treasures (page 137)

This is my version of a Jewish story, often attributed to Rabbi Nachman of Bratzlav. A very similar story is told in England as "The Peddler of Swaffham," in which a poor peddler lives in a house with a cherry tree in front, and dreams of a bridge in London. He travels there, findng nothing, but learns of a guard's dream, which sends him back to find that the treasure he sought was buried under his very own tree.

All these stories express one of the great themes in folklore: returning home to find what you had not seen before. I first learned of the story from my father.

The Strawberry (page 156)

Attributed to the Buddha, this is a classic Zen tale—very short, with an ending that may sound unresolved to a Western mind. Like Zen koans, these stories are meant to open up the listener's heart and mind.

I first learned of this story from the book *Zen Flesh, Zen Bones: A Collection of Zen and Pre-Zen Writings,* compiled by Paul Reps (Anchor Books, 1989).

Hershel's Last Laugh (page 171)

A literary cousin to Mullah Nasrudin, Hershel of Ostropol was an actual person, though many of the stories are undoubtedly apocryphal. An early stand-up comedian, he served as the official court jester to Rabbi Baruch of Medzibozh, the grandson of the great storyteller, Rabbi Israel, the Baal Shem Tov. According to legend, Rabbi Baruch lacked the wisdom of his grandfather and appointed Hershel to distract from his many mistakes. This, itself, turned out to be a mistake, as Hershel spent the rest of his life making Rabbi Baruch the butt of his jokes.

As with the Chelm stories, I first learned of Hershel from my mother's references.

The Happy Man's Shirt (page 180)

This story, which was originally told about Alexander the Great in the Greek literary work *Pseudo Callisthenes*, was popular in medieval times. Many variations exist around the world, including a Jewish version from Afghanistan and a Danish version, which became the basis for Hans Christian Andersen's story "The Shoes of Happiness."

The version in this book is adapted from several tales, including one, collected in Italy in 1912, from a housewife by the name of Orsola Minon, which appears in Italo Calvino's book, *Italian Folktales* (Pantheon, 1981). I learned of the background of the story from *Wisdom Tales From Around the World* by Heather Forest (August House, 1996).

The Fox in the Garden (page 193)

Many variations of this tale are known, including one of Aesop's Fables and a tale collected by the Brothers Grimm, in which a wolf overeats in a smokehouse and cannot escape through the same hole he had entered. Other versions have been found in Hawaii, Italy, and throughout Africa.

The double bind in this story, where the fox must first fast to enter, then fast again to leave the garden, seems to be a peculiarly Jewish twist. I first heard the tale at my father's funeral, from Rabbi Frank Ackerman, esq.

The Secret of Happiness (page 206)

Arguably the most famous trickster in the world, Nasrudin is known in the folklore of the Middle East, North Africa, India, and China. He goes by many names, including Hodja, Hoca, Khaji, Jocha, or simply Mullah, which is Persian for teacher. Though his stories are often secular, they are most treasured by Sufis, the mystical sect of Islam.

Although many countries claim to be his home, he is generally believed to have been born in Turkey, sometime around the year 1208. Legend has it that he is buried there, in a grave that has a heavily locked gate, but with no fence around it.

I first heard "The Secret of Happiness" from Elisheva Hart, a puppeteer and storyteller in San Francisco.

ACKNOWLEDGMENTS

I began this book thinking of writing as a solitary pursuit. This could not have been farther from the truth. It has only been through the efforts of many talented and generous people that I have been able to tell my tale. I am deeply grateful to the following: Jane Anne Staw; Rand Pallock; Rich Fettke; Jerry and Loreli Sontag; Mark Pinsky and Jennifer Paget; Rob Saper; Andrew Hasse; Zahava Sherez; Susan Helmrich; Frances Dinkelspiel; Josephine Coatsworth; Mary Mackey; Chris Ritter; fellow fathers Brett Weinstein, Rick Goldsmith, Dave Fariello, and David Hershcopf; Ruth Halpern; Sharon and Peter Leyden; Mark Berger; Miriam Attia; Kelly Miller and Ranu Pandey; Rachel and David Biale; Sid Ganis and Nancy Hult Ganis; Adrianne Bank; my cousin, Cindy Wedel; my aunt, Norma Glad; and to Rabbi Jack Riemer, who graciously permitted me to reprint his story. My appreciation as well to Green Gulch Farm Zen Center, for opening its doors to me when I needed a peaceful and quiet place to write.

Both academics and storytellers have been helpful in researching "About the Stories," and I am indebted to Professors Alan Dundes of the University of California, Berkeley, and Elliott Oring of California State University, Los Angeles. My thanks also to Ruth Stotter, Pleasant DeSpain, Heather Forest, and Howard Schwartz, and to the librarians at the Berkeley Public Library, for their help in tracking down the origins of stories.

I am thankful to my agent, Barbara Lowenstein, who first envisioned the book that lay buried within my story. She passed the mantle of agentry on to Dorian Karchmar, and I have been blessed by her wisdom and compassion every step of the way.

Everyone at Algonquin has welcomed this book with open arms. Elisabeth Scharlatt and Ina Stern, publisher and associate publisher, provided insight and guidance exactly when needed, while Antonia Fusco, my editor, took on the daunting task of helping this first-time author figure out which parts of the story to include and which to omit. To this challenge she brought vision, tenacity, and good judgment.

Some people have given me gifts that call for special mention: my parents, for passing on to me a love of story; my children, Elijah and Michaela, for providing the constant inspiration that let me tell this one; and my in-laws, Hezi and Ruthie, for their solidity and belief in me. I am particularly indebted to my great friend and writing partner, Jeff Lee, who provided a wellspring of advice and encouragement that kept me going. Finally, my thanks to Taly, a true woman of valor, who not only stood by my side through the challenges described in this book, but also through the writing of it. This she did with unwavering support, love, and editorial acumen, for which I am deeply grateful.